MEMOIR OF A FIRE CHIEF

Cover photo republished with permission of the *South Florida Sun Sentinel.*

Sparr, Jim
Memoir of a Fire Chief
ISBN 978-0-578-64599-5

Also for sale in ebook format: ISBN 978-0-578-64598-8

1. Biography & Autobiography / Personal Memoirs
2. Biography & Autobiography / Fire & Emergency Services

Assembled and polished by Bryan Tomasovich

Printed in the U.S.A.

MEMOIR OF A FIRE CHIEF

Jim Sparr

CONTENTS

*In my life, I've seen the transition from black & white to color photographs, I'm happy to say. All photos herein, except those from my youth, can be viewed in full color with bonus backstory on each at **jimsparr.com**.*

A politician, who liked bullying public servants, often complained about my shoe choice.

This photograph, to his disgust, earned me the nickname "Chief Reebok."

I dedicate *Memoir of a Fire Chief* episodes to my family and friends, as well as the women and men of the Wichita and the Fort Lauderdale Fire Departments. I think about these moments when I hear "My Thanksgiving," one of Don Henley's best songs; the lyrical poetry has three fire references all containing double meanings.

I disagree with the boat's name on the cover. I think life's interesting, and all you have to do is pay attention. A special thank-you to the *South Florida Sun Sentinel* for permission to republish the cover photograph.

To all emergency personnel: think health and safety.

1

CAREER SEARCH

In June of 1967, I joined the Wichita Fire Department. Throughout my career I never understood people who ran past me on their way out of a burning building as I ran inside. Didn't they understand how they'd just left danger and an accompanying adrenaline rush? Crawling with a hose line in total darkness under extreme stress while controlling one's inner physiological and mental reactions was an experience I wouldn't miss. A chance for a possible lifesaving rescue always existed. The Holy Grail, that is, a rescue, validated one's personal and professional worth in society.

I often expressed that worth in answer to the common question: "What do you do?"

"Why, I fight fire, save lives and property. What do you do?" That greeting worked equally well with condescending people and interesting women.

As a young firefighter, I concentrated on the Holy Grail. My duty and obligation later shifted from saving citizens' lives to saving the hero firefighters' lives. By focusing on saving firefighters' lives, my administration ended up saving more citizens' lives as well.

That summer the local aircraft economy rolled along because of the Vietnam War. Private aircraft manufacturing and all their parts suppliers kept busy, as did the military manufacturing. The major aircraft companies, Beech, Cessna, Learjet, and Boeing, all tried filling vacancies.

With the aircraft business booming, the rest of Wichita's economy also boomed because it followed the up-and-down cycle of the aircraft industry. Although public-sector jobs were plentiful, competition from the private sector created some difficulty in filling those vacancies. The federal government provided some funds for training fire and police personnel. Those funds also covered payroll support during the training period.

I was also recently divorced from my high school girlfriend, whom I'd married due to a surprise pregnancy during my first semester of college at Wichita State University. I had dropped out of college to support our new family. But I eventually agreed with my wife that we were both too young; the marriage lasted only eighteen months but produced a precious brown-eyed baby girl, Shelley. Like many divorced fathers of that era, I saw my daughter on weekends but spent too much time on job-related activities. My daughter and I lost time together that an intact family provides for such a bond. I still look at pictures of her at age two, not long after the divorce. My mother took one picture that showed me holding Shelley as she kissed my left cheek. I cherish it. My daughter eventually succeeded where I failed, in the area of marriage, because each generation rebels in different ways. Maybe my failures in marriage hold the key to why I worked so hard at succeeding with my fire department family.

§

I spent the first seven years of my life in Joplin, Missouri, a beautiful little community in the Bible Belt, near the borders of Kansas and Arkansas. It was a place where families attended church regularly, worked, played, and lived happily ever after. I was an only child until age seven. That's when we adopted my baby sister, Jeanie, from the Baptist hospital in Saint Louis. My father worked at the *Joplin Globe* as a newspaper pressman after he came home from World War II. He had served as a naval radio operator. Mom was a devoted full-time mother and homemaker. She managed the household budget, stretched dollars like they were made from rubber, and pinched pennies until President Lincoln screamed. She always prepared meals that made leftovers taste fresh. My favorite breakfast, biscuits and gravy, would turn up later as gravy on toast with shaved meat from still another meal. As I was growing up, marriage and family life seemed so easy, predictable, and orderly. Here I found myself, though, at age twenty, divorced, with financial obligations.

To financially start over after the divorce, I worked two full-time jobs. I had often worked two jobs, but not two full-time ones. I worked first shift at the Cessna Aircraft Company, clocked out, drove across town, and work second shift at the Boeing Aircraft Company. From there I went to my apartment and got about four and a half hours of sleep before heading back to my first-shift job.

My original employment began with Boeing, on the day shift, as a matériel coordinator. My responsibility started with a stack of paperwork identifying parts or assemblies. Each document had an ink-stamp marking that identified the individual part's importance. Aircraft parts or assemblies made their journey through design, engineering, manufacturing, engineered testing, assembly, and shipping. During that routing journey through acres of buildings with wide aisles and work areas bordered by yellow safety paint, the paperwork noted a final destination.

Stamped marks ranging from "important" to "priority" to "urgent" indicated the need for timely processing. A successful processing inquiry started with observing people and their perceived stations in life.

When interacting with work groups, I never began with "Have you seen this part?" Most of them could care less but did appreciate respect and humor.

I always began with "Exactly what do you do here?"

I learned a lot, and fellow workers displayed pride in their skills. Pride and humor were two primary ingredients for successful work groups. Later, that proved true in fire stations as well.

Sometimes my plant travels called for the use of a yellow three-wheeled scooter with a small bed for carrying parts. Instead of a pretty color like fire-engine red, the scooters had ugly yellow safety paint, but the color stood out, making them safer when navigating aisles.

The scooter trip out to the flight line became my favorite journey. While a guard activated the street-crossing light, I stared at the B-52 bombers with their long downward-sloping wings heavy from the weight of powerful jet engines. Most of them lined up with their tails pointing toward the runways. Some parked off to the side with blast fences behind them. Horizontal, slatted metal fence rails set apart at forty-five-degree angles redirected the engine exhaust blast upward when engine testing.

On one particular trip, I met Ted, an electronics engineer. Instead of answering my usual question, he asked, "Would you like to see what I do?"

Since it involved climbing inside the aircraft, I said, "Hell yes."

We made our way to the tail-gunner section of the aircraft. Ted explained everything about the enclosed tail section with an engineer's thoroughness. Then we got down to business. Ted's job was to ensure that the tail guns properly tracked enemy aircraft. He calibrated a tracking system by locking on F-4 Phantom jets taking off and landing on the adjacent McConnell Air Force Base runway. The fifty-caliber machine-gun barrels moved with the trajectory of each plane. I closed my eyes and imagined enemy aircraft meeting their demise with fifty-caliber slugs ripping through sheet-metal skins, causing smoke, fire, and a downward death spiral. Although I appreciated my employment, occasionally I escaped to such visions because I didn't have many adventuresome moments in my job.

In addition to a well-paying job, Boeing provided opportunities for trade education. I chose blueprint-reading classes, which served me well throughout my life. My second-shift transfer allowed participation in the trade classes, and that transfer allowed me to start work at Cessna on the first shift.

I pulled that off for a few months before supervision at Boeing caught me and requested a supervisor-employee conference. That conference seemed important because my line supervisor didn't go with me. I went to the big tan-brick administration building across the street.

People in this building wore different-colored badge banners with laminated names and pictures, with "Administration" carved in their plastic clipped-on name badges attached to a shirt or jacket pocket. A secretary walked me to a large room filled with gray metal desks and no partitions. She pointed at a man and told me, "Have a seat in the chair next to his desk." Management supervisor "Doc" Loveland had a grandfatherly appearance and began our discussion by informing me that Boeing had a policy against working for other aircraft companies. He then stated, "You need to leave Cessna."

After listening to my story of needing a maximum income, Doc understood that I appreciated the continued Boeing employment opportunity, but Cessna offered ten-hour days and some weekend work. Those extra hours with overtime pay would help me reach my goals sooner.

I left Boeing and began working for Cessna as "Jimmy the Riveter." The famous "Rosie the Riveter" from World War II inspired me. A smile always came across my face when co-workers complained about ten-hour days and weekend work. I enjoyed having almost as much total income and getting as many as six hours of sleep, if necessary. I only got six hours of sleep because of my two new skills, carousing and chasing women. As I honed these favored skills, attention to my work as a sheet metal mechanic began to wane from lack of sleep and boredom.

The most memorable example of my waning came when I drilled a rivet hole with an eighth-inch drill bit through two pieces of metal. Because of the awkward and time-consuming effort in using a clamp, I held the pieces together with my fingers. The task required holding a reinforcing metal clip against a metal support rib of a plane with my less dominant hand, while drilling through both pieces of the metal with my dominant hand. As in previous jobs, I searched for adventurous opportunities.

My challenge became doing that task quickly. From an initial trigger pull to letting off when a drill bit exited the second piece of metal took two seconds. That rivet hole, in particular, was a masterpiece because I drilled it perfectly. The only problem occurred when my left index finger, which held the metal clip, didn't move over. The left and right hands hadn't communicated. I drilled through both pieces of metal and my left index finger, exiting through my fingernail.

I noticed what happened right away. I saw my finger skewered on the drill bit. The time had arrived for meaningful reflection while lying on my back in the tail section of an airplane.

When I had graduated from Wichita North High School in 1964, I stood five feet six inches, with a lean, muscular build, and weighed 145 pounds. In the three years since, I had gained three inches in height and put on ten more pounds. I still retained my high degree of natural flexibility, which made accessing the narrowing tunnel of a tail section easy. The coffin-like enclosure, however, meant that nobody could help me. The time for self-reliance, as instilled by my parents, also arrived. Letting go of the drill would break the drill bit off. Since my co-workers couldn't climb inside, they would take a long time removing a sheet metal section. Then a team would begin deliberations on extracting my wayward finger. That wouldn't be good for the company, or my finger, which felt remorseful pain for what happened.

Only two options remained. I could place the high-speed air drill in reverse with my thumb. Variable speed drills didn't exist at the time, which meant a bit would back out quickly. My left forefinger lobbied for that option. That option would do more tissue and fingernail damage as the spiral cutting edges of the drill bit that separated nerve and flesh tissue released its contents. The other option involved holding the drill chuck (drill bit holder) with my right thumb and forefinger while cradling the drill with my remaining three fingers and slowly backing it out by hand. That option, although causing less tissue and nail damage, would take more time. A high pain tolerance made me prefer a lot of pain quickly, rather than the boredom of less pain over more time. I chose a hybrid of the two options.

I pressed the reverse button and quickly backed the drill bit out with my right thumb and forefinger. The nerve endings of my fingernail bed reminded me, with each quarter turn, of the mistake my finger made. I climbed out of the plane and went to a first aid station for an application of disinfectant and a Band-Aid. The drill bit missed the bone, so no permanent damage had resulted from the mistake, with about one hour of lost productive time.

I called events like that *tuition*. Pay attention, learn, and move on. Workplace accidents (mistakes) and prevention of the same would be the hallmarks of my future career.

That body-piercing mistake could've been prevented, thereby causing no harm to me and no lost productive time for my employer. That mistake would pale in comparison, however, to my ultimate failure in providing an honest day's work for a fair wage. Investing more time in hedonistic activities and searching for a new mate caused the need for more rest. What better sleeping place than on the job?

Even though Cessna manufactured private aircraft, the need existed for military planes. My group worked on retrofitting T-37 trainer jets for the military. We focused on the stripped-down body of an aircraft mounted on a jig with wheels that moved along an assembly line. The jets had side-by-side seating in the cockpits. A thick plastic bubble canopy enclosed a cockpit and rotated partially open like a car convertible top. Co-workers installed new engines, and I strengthened support ribs in the tail sections. Other retrofitting took place, but my world revolved around placing reinforcing clips on the support ribs of a tail section. The tail section needed strengthening because of structural stress caused by new, more powerful engines.

I shed a little of my guilt for not serving in the military by believing my job efforts helped. My draft designation because of my bad knees, the result of high school gymnastics injuries, probably kept me from being drafted. Anything I did for the war effort seemed insignificant compared to what others were doing. Several of my high school classmates didn't come back from Vietnam alive.

I read blueprints and had a medium build. That combination, along with my high degree of flexibility, provided what I had arrogantly thought was a tenured position doing what others couldn't or wouldn't do.

To access a tail section, I entered from the plane's belly, rolled over on my back, and slowly wiggled over support ribs toward the tail section's narrowing tunnel. The actual work occurred in a confined space. As long as a tail cone cap remained attached, nobody could see me. Perfect! I caught a nice short nap.

Sometimes a tail cone cap was off, which allowed a supervisor to check on an employee and see if they needed anything. Unfortunately, an open portal also enabled a supervisor to see a motionless body. The first time my supervisor called my name he asked, "Are you okay?"

"My arms are tired from working overhead. I just finished resting them."

The second time my supervisor gave me a warning. The third time he didn't say much. He brought a wiry guy in from second shift who read blueprints. I should've seen it coming. I soon departed.

By that time in 1967, at age twenty, I had money in the bank and a nice set of wheels. I enjoyed running around all night and resting by the apartment complex pool during the day. Then a chance encounter with an off-duty firefighter, also working on his tan, turned my professional life around.

Midweek meant few people gathered around the pool. As I took my seat on a lounge chair facing the sun, another lone tanner glanced up. We nodded to each other and started bronzing.

After a few moments, I asked, "Do you live in the complex?"

He grinned. "No, I only stopped by to swim and tan."

I appreciated honesty and boldness.

After confirming my legal occupancy, the trespassing acquaintance introduced himself. "I'm Mike."

"I'm Jim."

"What do you do?"

"Nothing now," I replied, and I explained my recent firing and newfound freedom, tempered by the contemplation of a dwindling bank account. "What do you do?"

"I'm a firefighter."

Mike began telling me about his job and the recruiting process.

It all sounded intriguing, and then he mentioned the work hours: twenty-four hours on duty and twenty-four hours off. I sat transfixed as the next words came out of his mouth. After a moment of stunned silence, I asked, "Would you slowly repeat what you just said?"

"After 8:00 p.m., barring fire alarms, you can sleep until 6:55 a.m."

I applied the next day.

2

SEARCH OVER

To have a larger candidate pool, the Wichita Fire Department (WFD) lowered the minimum age requirement from twenty-one to eighteen and relaxed the five-foot-nine-inch minimum height requirement and the 160-pound minimum weight requirement. Attracting more candidates worked, although some said we didn't attract the best and brightest. Yes, those comments applied to me as well.

The mechanical aptitude test with pictures of pulleys and attached belts required a candidate to identify the direction of pulley travel. The time I spent working with equipment made the test easy. Then came the psychological questionnaire. The following week, after reviewing my notification of a required doctor's appointment, I headed out to the swimming pool.

The next morning while driving to the health department, I wondered what the physical examination covered. I became a little suspicious when a receptionist directed me to the mental health section of the department and down a hall to room 105. Room 105 didn't have an examination table, only a desk and bookshelf. The doctor sat at his desk studying some papers. He glanced up at me, then back at his papers and asked for my name. After confirming my identity, he said, "Have a seat next to my desk." The doctor wasn't wearing a lab coat and didn't have a stethoscope around his neck. "I've been reviewing your questionnaire answers." After a few moments, he looked up at me. "Do you have a strong religious background?"

"I do."

"Tell me about your first church memory."

I thought about my father. He was a deacon in the church, a World War II veteran, and hardworking. Although he had a gentle nature, Dad seemed more serious than Mom, but that probably stemmed from how he saw his family role. Mom always flittered about finding humor anywhere she paused. She always laughed at my struggle against Sunday morning dress-up. Dad carried the moniker "Big Jim," and I was "Little Jim." Mom said, "Little Jim, clothes make the man." Dad always nodded in agreement. To this day, I hate formal clothing and look suspiciously for the substance behind a person's tidy appearance.

I paused for a moment, then answered the PhD's question.

"After my parents left my Kansas birthplace, we moved to Joplin, Missouri. My first memory of church occurred at the Friendship Baptist Church. I must've been about five years old, and apparently acted up during a Sunday morning service. My father usually gave me an initial warning sign in the form of a stare. His intense stare made one of my heroes, Clint Eastwood, look like a rosy-cheeked choirboy. I must've been too busy being cute because I missed it."

"What happened next?"

I told him how my father gently picked me up and headed down the aisle toward the front exit. "As my mother tells the story, I knew a spanking was in my immediate future and started crying loudly, 'Don't hurt that baby.'"

"How did the congregation react?"

"As my mother put it, 'Today your performance might have worked, but then there was only hushed amusement throughout the faithful flock.'"

I told the doctor I didn't remember acting up in church again but did remember keeping an eye open for that stare.

"Tell me about the next religious event you remember."

"That was an old-fashioned tent revival. I must've been about seven years old.

"The revivals began with preachers who traveled country roads, set up tents, passed out brochures, and delivered hellfire and damnation sermons on the advertised day. Preachers who delivered the most emotion with their sermons had larger crowds, as they tried to 'revive' sinners, hence the name 'tent revivals.'

"The one gathering I remember featured a preacher who got so worked up, he turned red in the face. Sweat poured from his forehead.

He had my attention. As he held the Bible in one hand and wiped sweat from his brow with the other, he told me I was going to hell if I didn't confess my sins and ask for God's forgiveness. I couldn't think of anything to confess but knew some action was required. Not long afterward, I sat in a Sunday service at the Friendship Baptist Church, listening to Reverend Moudy talk about a loving God and how easily I could be saved. Shortly thereafter I accepted Jesus Christ into my life, but my motivation came from the fear the traveling preacher instilled."

"Please continue."

"After Joplin, my father, mother, recently adopted baby sister, Jeanie, and I moved to Wichita, Kansas, and joined the Olivet Baptist Church. I remained with that church, participating every Sunday morning, Sunday night, and Wednesday night for Bible study until the age of sixteen. I even considered being a preacher, complete with a tryout sermon at age fifteen in the Calvary Baptist Church located on West Maple Street."

"Why didn't you continue on that career path?"

"I simply felt that I couldn't live the kind of life expected of a preacher."

He smiled as if to say, *Now we are getting somewhere.*

I asked him, "Why do you want to know about my religious background?"

"After looking over your questionnaire, I thought I was about to meet Jesus Christ, but after you explained your background, I understand what occurred. To all the questions related to lying, stealing, and cheating you answered no. Have you ever lied, stolen, or cheated?"

"Of course."

"Why didn't you answer yes to the questions?"

"The questions didn't ask if I had ever lied, stolen, or cheated, but do I lie, steal, or cheat? Although I have technically lied, cheated, and stolen in my life, I don't do those things as a matter of course. My lessons at church, and reinforced at home, taught me not to lie, cheat, or steal. Lying, like swearing, let me savor a bar of soap in my mouth. Cheating by stealing a look at a Christmas present deprived me of my use of that present until the day after Christmas. Besides, I'm applying for a job, and I'm not going to say that I'm a routine liar or thief."

The PhD then switched focus from our fifty-question questionnaire to another with one hundred questions and took me to another room. "Fill this one out and remember our conversation."

I completed the questionnaire, and every time a question came up about lying, cheating, or stealing, I answered yes.

He reviewed my answers and looked at me in a professorial manner. "Would you have any difficulty working with men who use foul language?"

"Hell no."

"Report to personnel, and they will give you instructions for the oral interview process." I found out later the PhD was looking for people who weren't perfect, squeamish, or sensitive because management thought those were reasons for employee turnover.

The WFD held the oral interviews at Fire Station 2. I parked behind the two-story dark-redbrick building and entered through one of the open garage doors.

A firefighter greeted me. "Are you here for your interview?"

"Yes. Am I in the right building?"

The firefighter pointed at two open side-by-side dark-green interior doors. "Take those stairs, turn left at the top, and wait in the game room."

In the game room, a couple of other applicants sat in chairs around the Ping-Pong table. I leaned against the pool table until someone called my name.

I entered the office and sat in a chair facing three officers across a desk. They asked me questions like "Why do you want to be a firefighter?" With the psych test still fresh in my memory, I didn't mention the sleeping thing because lying seemed okay. I gave answers like "I like to help people."

That was true because my church and parents ingrained that in me. Anytime a church member, neighbor, or even a stranger needed help, my parents always provided that help in any way possible.

I passed my interview and received only one suggestion. My height was okay, but my weight at 155 pounds caused some concern. An officer commented, "If you eat a lot of bananas and drink beer, you'll gain weight quickly." That same stunned silence came over me as it did that day by the pool.

"I will do my best."

Personnel had me report to the WFD training facility north of the Boeing Company.

From the age of twelve on I worked as a paperboy, lawn mower, dairy farm hand, butcher shop helper, metal display-rack fabricator, wheel stop installer for Beech aircraft, assistant fountain and grill manager, milkman, matériel coordinator for Boeing, sheet metal mechanic for Cessna, painter, and carpenter. I even took flying lessons in a Beechcraft Musketeer to become a pilot and soloed after nine hours, but on my second touch-and-go bounced hard on the landing. An air traffic controller radioed and asked, "Are you okay?"

"Ten-four, just a matter of stupidly flying too slow."

I thought about taxiing in and quitting but called myself a gutless coward, gave the engine full throttle, and became airborne for one more fly-around. That time I maintained a proper airspeed and accomplished a perfect landing. I taxied over to a ramp parking space, climbed out, and never went back.

I briefly considered becoming a dentist until auditing a chemistry class. Of course, part of the required study for a rookie firefighter involved the chemistry of fire, but by that time understanding and enjoyment kept me motivated. I always wanted a job I looked forward to every workday and eagerly anticipated returning to after vacation. Within eight weeks my search for the perfect career would be over.

Sunday Best

3

GET LOW AND GO

The 240 hours of required training occurred over a six-week period Monday through Friday from 8:00 a.m. to 5:00 p.m. Only one other rookie in my class remained on the job to retirement age. Higher-paying private-sector jobs, not the PhD's failed character profile in our psych interviews, created a high turnover rate. The fire department shifts of twenty-four hours on and twenty-four hours off remained attractive because of the time available for second jobs. Later, city management meddled with the twenty-four-hour shifts, then wondered why yet another turnover problem arose. Also, contentious labor relations and lack of employee appreciation created an environment perfect for a labor strike. During entry-level training, though, the challenges kept all rookies motivated.

The training grounds consisted of a huge concrete area with a five-story steel skeleton structure. That structure had three open sides and one closed for simulating structural firefighting operations. Training officers could observe tactical operations on any floor. The closed side had windows cut out where we practiced rappelling and other operations. A concrete pit filled with water allowed drafting (suctioning water) by pumpers, for testing and certifying pumps on fire trucks. We practiced drafting because that method would be used in areas without fire hydrants, if a pond, lake, or river was available. Of course, the training grounds had a functioning fire hydrant.

We had a "smokehouse," where burning straw in a chamber on one end resulted in white smoke filling the enclosed structure. Training officers used that smoke-filled environment for simulating actual fire conditions and hid a large dummy at various locations inside the structure. Training officers had rookies crawl into the structure, find the dummy, and drag or carry it to safety. That simulation exercise allowed for acclimation in a smoke-filled and claustrophobic environment. In that type of environment, firefighters couldn't see one inch in front of their faces because of total darkness. Fire scenes in movies are phony. Directors who focus so much on visual images have no clue how to portray a much more dramatic aspect of firefighting. They don't use the frustrated sounds of muffled communication through air masks, the low-volume groans from instant heat that penetrated exposed skin like ears, or the whooshing sound of a backdraft fire that flew above one's body and potentially blocked a firefighter's escape. All those experiences happened in total darkness without visual images.

A hostile, claustrophobic, and confusing environment made for interesting reactions in all rookie classes. We all had the same training, but individual reactions varied. That training exercise washed out some rookies. Some didn't like the smoke that clung to our baggy white overalls and hair. Others just got scared. Although it didn't happen in our class, occasionally a story circulated about some rookie who didn't come back from lunch. Some firefighters labeled those rookies as cowards. I always thought of them as people who made a good decision because I imagined what would've happened if they'd panicked in a situation where a teammate needed them.

Trainers sent us into a simulated burning structure with teammates. Fire departments ingrained recruits with the team concept and reinforced that once employees were assigned to a station. Firefighters trained together, fought fire together, ate together, and shared large common bunkrooms. In most departments, they worked together twenty-four hours a day. As part of actual firefighting, we usually entered dangerous environments in teams of two or more for task completion and safety if one got into trouble. These were reasons why firefighters developed into family-like groups. That's also why firefighters often die in multiple numbers; this explains some of the 9/11 horrors.

While attempting a training rescue, we tied a rope around our waists, and a teammate stayed by an entrance, keeping a tight line. When we entered a hostile environment, we dropped to our knees and crawled. We systematically crawled around a room's perimeter, sweeping left and right with our hands, feeling for a dummy, which, in real life, would be a person.

In training and afterward, as we entered a hostile environment for fighting a fire, we found the enemy and extinguished it. We always carried a fire hose with us. If we got lost or disoriented, we followed a hose line back out. We took a hose line and crawled into a structure because both heat and smoke rose. If a fire hadn't burned for long, smoke didn't extend down to the floor. Occasionally we saw a distinct layer of semi-clear atmosphere near a floor. We wore a self-contained breathing apparatus, and if our air tanks ran dry, that bottom layer of clearer atmosphere might provide cooler and more breathable air.

Training officers taught us the use of hearing and feeling when locating the enemy, and I remembered those training techniques later in my career. A crackling and popping sound like that heard around a campfire led me to several flames. In a couple of fires, I found the origin of heat by pulling a glove off a bit and using my exposed wrist as a heat direction indicator. Sometimes a roaring fire-breathing monster made its location quite clear, and we slew it because we were the invincible warriors chosen specifically for that calling.

During any operation, we remained next to the floor. I have witnessed fire fatalities that would not have occurred if the victims had only gone to the floor and crawled out. They naturally stood up and ran. That panicked behavior, coupled with rapid and deep breathing, has caused many fire fatalities. The fire didn't kill people. Breathing superheated gases that can enter the lungs with as little as one or two breaths can cause death. That's the reason unsung heroes in fire prevention have come up with public education sayings like "Get low and go."

My training officers also taught another technique—controlled breathing. Controlled breathing, with or without an air tank and mask, has two purposes. First, shallow, controlled breathing allows the air in our tanks to last longer. A hostile and dark environment can cause rapid and deep breathing, coupled with a more rapid heart rate. Both during training and in countless real-life situations I've heard other firefighters' rapid, heavy breathing. Some could suck a fifteen-minute air tank dry in seven and one-half minutes. Air tanks have an alarm bell that sounds when our air supply runs low. Firefighters then leave a structure, no longer of use to the team and endangering themselves. Those hostile and dark environments always reaffirmed my career choice of excitement and challenge.

The second purpose of controlled breathing involves calming our bodies so our minds can concentrate on a task at hand. If a panic occurs, firefighters forget their training and task assignment like the washed-out rookies did in training. Panic can be contagious. If a company officer in charge panics, a team also panics. Group panic can occur with all people, not only emergency personnel. Observe what happens to some financial investors during sudden economic downturns without life-threatening situations. People who know how to think pay attention, remain calm, and then make critical decisions.

At the training center, in addition to a training tower and smokehouse, a corrugated blue-metal facility housed a small classroom that adjoined vehicle bays, where the older pumpers were used for training. A pumper, the vehicle most associated with firefighters, pumped water through fire hose lines. Our "hands-on" training occurred in and around the training tower.

We studied in a classroom without air-conditioning. If training officers had some downtime between training modules, we studied our "red" book.

That book contained almost all the information we needed over the next year for passing our probationary exam. During study time, rookies read and sometimes studied the red book. June and July in Wichita with no air-conditioning didn't create a good environment for learning. The mornings were tolerable, but heat buildup from the previous day lingered and intensified as concrete surfaces warmed. Although wind blew every afternoon, a slight and hot breeze that came through an open window provided little relief.

While in training we worked eight-hour days, so I spent my evenings and weekends on my suggested weight-gain program and even had an occasional banana. That result became apparent during afternoon book-reading sessions when other rookies and I drifted off into dreams of single-handedly extinguishing large fires. This time daydreaming didn't provide an escape, but rather the anticipation of welcomed danger and successful task assignment. We looked out for each other because that's what firefighters do. One day while on watch, I saw a training officer heading for the classroom and awakened two guys. "Hang on, boys; we're only two weeks away from our dream job." That day came quickly, and we all received our station assignments.

All my training at that point involved the "what to think" type of training, like setting ladders, tying knots, stretching hose lines, or applying a minimal amount of water. The success of firefighting teamwork required that individuals perform tasks in the same way.

For safety's sake, always set a ladder one-quarter of the ladder's height from a structure. Stay low out of rising heat, and squirt water at a fire's base so that the resultant steam helps extinguishment.

Years would pass by before a first promotion, so any knowledge on "how to think" came from observing others. Ignoring behavior that didn't work and cataloging what worked for different firefighters and officers began about that stage in my career. It's possible that's when I started thinking about someday becoming an officer, but at the time, following the herd mentality ruled. I received my assignment to Station 2, 500 South Topeka.

4

VERBAL VOLLEYBALL

Wichita had three fire districts in 1967 and two shifts, then later three shifts. Each district contained three supposedly equal land areas with five stations each. A district chief managed captains at those stations, and captains managed lieutenants and personnel in stations that had more than one fire vehicle. District chiefs reported to the deputy chief of operations, who reported to a fire chief. My assignment sent me to District 2, Fire Station 2, located at 500 South Topeka near downtown. Station 2, a two-story dark-redbrick building, had concrete keystones over the windows and doors and four front garage bay doors. With six fire vehicles and sixteen personnel, it was the largest of five stations in District 2.

The sixteen personnel at Station 2 included a district chief, a captain, three lieutenants, and eleven firefighters. Fire departments considered each fire vehicle and assigned personnel a firefighting company. My station assignment let me watch all the interaction between pumper and ladder companies. In addition to any victim rescue potential, ladder companies provided ventilation. Ventilation allowed smoke out of a structure and a clearer atmosphere in its place for an interior attack by pumper companies.

Naturally, a flare-up occurred with the introduction of fresh air (oxygen) to a heat and fuel mixture, the three components for fire. That's why ladder companies waited for placement of fire hose lines before ventilating. Besides companies interacting, personnel and different ranks interacting required the most attention. Officers, like firefighters, had unique characteristics. Recognizing differences and communicating accordingly determined one's level of acceptance on a team. By observing those interactions, I coined a saying: "Life is interesting—all you have to do is pay attention."

Great anticipation and excitement filled my first duty day with thoughts focusing on new co-workers. I arrived at work forty-five minutes early because training officers had taught me three important protocols. First, all good firefighters carry a pocketknife because it can come in handy. I proudly produced my pocketknife to three inquiries that day. The third inquiry came from another firefighter, Bo, who had about two years on the job. He opened my knife blade and felt the cutting edge with his thumb. "So you don't look stupid trying to cut something, bring it to me after dinner tonight and I'll hone a good edge for you."

"Yes, sir."

"Don't call me sir. Save that for the officers. It makes them feel important. Chief officers wear white shirts, captains and lieutenants light blue. The real firefighters like you and me all wear gray."

"Okay. Thanks." I already knew that but didn't say so because I appreciated his advice.

The second protocol, the standard of showing up thirty to forty-five minutes early for reporting, had several purposes. That protocol let incoming firefighters check equipment like air tank bottles to make sure they had maximum pressure. It also allowed incoming firefighters to check in with firefighters going off duty to find out any pertinent information from the previous duty day. Most important, early reporting let incoming firefighters respond in the event of an alarm. Firefighters going off duty then left at 8:00 a.m. rather than waiting until returning from an alarm. That could save co-workers from being late for any days-off activities such as a second job or family obligations.

The third protocol stated that reputations are defined early in a career, so pay attention to number 2, early reporting. Firefighters who reported for duty close to 8:00 a.m. more than once received the nickname "Five-Minute Man." That label didn't sound like much, but it signaled that others would soon bring a Five-Minute Man back in line. If shunning didn't work, sometimes his relief reported to work early but didn't relieve the Five-Minute Man of duty until five minutes before 8:00 a.m., as he had done when he came on duty. A Five-Minute Man then sat pensively waiting for the "I gotcha" greeting. Occasionally an offending individual who didn't get the message got shipped out to a smaller station, where shunning became more focused and intense. The name "Five-Minute Man" had a different connotation in civilian life. Either way, I knew I didn't want that label.

Ex-military personnel filled many positions in the fire service. When troops came home from World War II, the Korean War, and Vietnam, they naturally gravitated to paramilitary organizations such as police and fire. Local governments even encouraged that by giving veterans extra consideration for hiring and promotions. From a local government point of view, that practice provided employees already trained in leadership, accountability, adaptability, communication skills, and organizational integrity. Employees with those qualities gave organizations a better chance at success. The net result became the foundation of paramilitary-style organizations. Many traditions remaining today, such as changing of the guard or roll call, can be traced back to those early foundations.

Roll call began when a dispatcher announced "8:00 a.m." twice over station speakers. Personnel lined up in descending order by rank and seniority. A station captain inspected firefighters and called the roll. That seemed pedantic to me because we easily saw everyone's presence. But I was part of the next generation of firefighters with no military service. For the first few months, everyone expected rookies to be seen but not heard. With five months under my belt, one day instead of answering, "Here," I answered, "Present."

When the station captain looked up from his logbook I finished the phrase, "Present for duty, sir," and we all moved on with my co-workers grinning. That began my quest to interject humor regardless of a situation.

After roll call, a station captain always provided any necessary information and work began. Drivers remained downstairs, checked their fire vehicles, and swept floors. Floor-sweeping in the bays or garage area began in the hose tower, where drying hose hung and a fifty-five-gallon drum contained a mixture of sawdust and linseed oil. Drivers spread that concoction across one end of the four vehicle bays and, using push brooms, moved it to the other end. That process picked up any loose debris and all the dust that accumulated from the previous twenty-four hours. Over the years oily residue sealed the concrete floors.

Saturday morning's cleanup differed from that of other days. On Saturday, drivers drove all vehicles outside onto the front and back concrete slabs for washing and a complete inventory. They scrubbed and mopped the bay floors. The only problem occurred when the floors became wet. When water stood on top of the oil-sealed concrete, the surface became slick. That's the reason drivers put their rubber-treaded fire boots on while scrubbing floors. If someone approached a wet floor from the outside or another area of the station, drivers said, "Red flag." That fascinated me because those two words told someone what to think about their surroundings—*danger*. How an individual thought and reacted decided whether they slipped and fell or stepped cautiously.

I always looked at situations, like wet floors, differently. Instead of avoiding danger, I contemplated fixing it, improving it, and interjecting laughter. One day I progressed from shuffling my leather-soled shoes to motions like ice-skating. That made the soles of my shoes wet, but decreased friction and let me slide further. I graduated from skating to starting outside on a full run. When I got to the wet floor and kept my balance, I slid a long way. (In the movie *Risky Business*, if Tom Cruise had only worn silk dress stockings instead of cotton socks, the outtakes would have been more interesting.)

A fellow firefighter saw me do this and tried it. He picked it up quickly. Let me provide an understatement: firefighters always compete. It doesn't matter if it involves cockroach racing, fire training exercises, or promotional examinations. So began our brief game of distance sliding. I kicked his butt until he learned my secret of wetting my soles first. About that time one of the "old heads," as we called them, never looked up from his mopping but uttered two words, "Red flag." That ended that.

While drivers worked on the ground floor, other firefighters cleaned the upstairs area. The upstairs consisted of a large bunkroom, restroom, showers, kitchen, district chief quarters, TV room, and a game room with a pool table and Ping-Pong table. The stairs and floors were concrete, with small white octagonal tiles in the restroom. The cleaning technique differed from the one downstairs. We used a long-handled push duster and, of course, mops. I got pretty good at both wet and dry mopping. Dry mopping ensured no streaking. We also cleaned the urinals, toilets, and sinks with Ajax. I learned that different officers concentrated on different areas of cleaning based on their wishes or experience.

Years later I worked for an obsessively detailed captain whose primary concern focused on the removal of Ajax residue from the bathroom sinks' front surfaces. Every morning after cleanup, he leaned against a sink and checked out his face. He didn't care about his face. Rather, when he stepped back and looked at his dark-blue uniform pants, there had better not be any white residue clinging to them. Any white residue on his pants guaranteed a lecture and more hands-on practice at other janitorial duties for the entire crew. If he stepped back and gazed at his spotless uniform pants, the day went swimmingly.

That's where I developed what I called the "Ajax theory of management," from a subordinate's point of view. A simple theory: pay attention. Find out a supervisor's main areas of concern and spend extra time on those.

I also paid attention to "shotgun discipline." That's when an entire group received verbal discipline because of one or two people. I thought it better if an officer focused on the individual(s) responsible for the transgressions. Others would hear about it and learn rather than feel falsely accused.

When I was a rookie at Station 2, morning school began after we cleaned the fire vehicles and station. A station captain or company lieutenants used a variety of training methods ranging from hands-on training to text material, to asking random addresses with respondents providing the fastest route to those addresses. Whatever method officers chose, the entire team participated. In addition to such continuing training, rookies like me not only read but studied the red book and hydrant locations in our response district.

Occasionally we had a roundtable discussion or "bitch session," where firefighters talked about anything. Later, I used that management technique in an open-door policy to maintain a sense of free speech and to allow firefighters to vent feelings. Firefighters vented their feelings all the time, but venting in a proper forum allowed for the free exchange of thoughts complete with responses. That kind of exchange helped stop rumors and built support for policies. If complaining occurred without full participation, rumors and accusations stood unchallenged. That hurt morale. Asking questions helped stop rumors and clarified policies.

One day as I sat in the kitchen while listening to the radio, a voice over all station speakers announced, "Sixty-six (upstairs) to the classroom. Today's subject will be a roundtable discussion."

Captain Seaman, a balding man with a long belt around his midsection, was someone I had known for years. I suspected he asked for my assignment to his station. He began the discussion by asking, "Who wants to start us off?"

Firefighter Klien, a tall, blond, blue-eyed firefighter, declared, "I think we are all becoming too janitorial-oriented." He made the point that we wasted time on a few specks of dust. He also suggested that some officers used a white glove inspection to justify their supervisory positions. That sounded right to me.

Shortly after that, as I pushed a dust mop around the bunkroom floor, Lieutenant Rob came in. He had more hair in his ears than on his head and a stout build, with large forearms and wrists. He cautioned, "Remember to dust under the bunks." I stood still staring at Lieutenant Rob. He waited for me to say something. Instead, I threw the dust mop to the floor, and the sound of the handle cracking against the concrete floor echoed in the bunkroom. Then I ran over to an open window and jumped up on top of a second-story windowsill.

"You didn't even listen to what we just discussed. I'm going to jump if you don't cut it out." When he didn't respond quickly enough, I jumped and caught my hands on the windowsill at the last moment.

He came running over. "Okay, okay, okay." I climbed back inside.

He laughed. "Don't do that. You will give me a heart attack." I grinned at first, and then we both burst into laughter.

I had known Captain Kendal Seaman since my preteen years from church and Lieutenant Rob knew that he shouldn't mess with Captain Seaman's golden boy. Later, he told the other officers what I did, and they all laughed. That puffed up my young ego and paved the way for other antics.

One such episode began when Lieutenant Rob said that his old truck couldn't possibly be flooded out. He made that claim after a series of heavy rains that left cars stranded.

My challenge to him was "I can flood it out with little water."

"No, you can't!"

After an obligatory Coke bet, I slid down the pole, took the station hose line, and opened up a torrent around his distributor cap. When Lieutenant Rob tried to start that old truck, a long time passed. The occasional slurping sound of a delicious soft drink grew louder while I watched the endeavor. Never one to gloat, I helped with a jump start when his battery gave out.

Since training officers provided individual information about rookies to their assigned station captains, I weighed in the first day. If a rookie was close to the 160-pound requirement, the issue never came up again. Based on that information, I quit drinking as much beer. I weighed in at 157 pounds.

"That's close enough," the company lieutenant said. "We will fatten you up with firehouse food." They didn't. My beer bloat left quickly, and within one week I went back to my fighting weight of 155 pounds.

"Forty-four" announced over station speakers signaled the lunch hour from noon to 1:00 p.m. Cooks provided legendary firehouse food, but I didn't understand until that first day. The designated cook, usually a private, purchased groceries for the meals and divided the cost equally among those in the "cooking clique." Belonging to the cooking clique wasn't mandatory; however, that group attempted to unravel the fabric of the team concept. Those who brought their own food or had it brought to them couldn't use any of the condiments purchased from clique money or touch any leftovers. Another unwritten rule prevented taking food that belonged to other shifts. I've been to other firefighting communities where hasps and locks placed on refrigerators prevented refrigerator wars. One-upping could get ugly!

Another culinary behavior I witnessed involved the art of slicing a pie. The unwritten rule stated that whoever ate the last piece washed the pan. I've seen remaining slices so thin one could read a newspaper through them.

Cooks got out of certain station duties in return for their culinary talents. While kidding, known as verbal volleyball, became a mainstay between firefighters, the cook was off-limits. At an earlier point in WFD history, some firefighter made a funny comment to a cook, in front of other firefighters for heightened ridicule. The cook walked over, picked up the offending firefighter's plate, discarded the contents in the trash, broke the plate, and threw it in the trash.

Legend had it that when a comment occurred before a meal, the cook walked over, picked up the offending firefighter's clean plate, broke it, and threw it in the trash. From that time on, if someone said something offensive to the cook, he merely asked, "Do you want a broken plate?" That ended the conversation, and everyone moved on quickly. When playing verbal volleyball, look for the spike. The broken-plate question noted a spike.

I enjoyed playing verbal volleyball. As someone volleyed cruder, ruder, and more insensitive words, I always responded, "I will play verbal volleyball with you, but you better get ready for the spike."

I'd even intervene on behalf of someone more timid. One incident occurred after morning roll call when an old head grilled a new rookie. He asked the rookie how many times he had sex on his recent wedding night.

"Once."

The old head scoffed. "I had sex four times on my wedding night." That would've been okay, but he wouldn't let up. "What's wrong, you couldn't go more than once?" The rookie became more and more flustered.

I finally interjected, "Did you ever stop to think that maybe his wife wasn't used to it?"

That broke the tension, and we all went our separate ways with my co-workers' mouths forming the letter *O*, confirming the spike.

All these episodes confirmed my career choice. I felt like part of a delightful new family with brothers.

5

REMAIN CALM

Firefighters always remember their first alarm response. Mine occurred the afternoon of my first duty day while studying and listening to other alarm responses over station radio speakers. Sometime in the late afternoon, I heard a station speaker click on. The dispatcher sounded two electronic tones and announced, "Still alarm for squad two, trash fire," and gave the address. Two tones and still alarm meant that only my pumper company would respond. The dispatcher repeated the message.

My heart rate increased as I slid down a fire pole, walked over to the pumper's back end, kicked off my shoes, and stepped into my boots. I put on my fire coat, helmet, and gloves, then stepped up on the tailboard. I pulled the safety belt around my waist, clicked it shut, and gave the thumbs-up to the lieutenant sitting in the cab's passenger seat. He looked back at me through the cab's rear window.

The driver started the motor, turned on the emergency lights, rolled out of the bay door, and turned left. As the truck began moving along, the lieutenant activated a wind siren with a foot switch. The foot switch was pressed intermittently and held down as we approached an intersection. When held down, a deafening high-pitched scream along with air horns moved cars out of the way. While en route, the lieutenant pulled out a district map and checked the alarm route along with the closest fire hydrant location because the address was out of our normal response district. I held on tight to a chrome grab-handle bar where the other end of my safety belt remained attached. As we headed east, we picked up speed. I thought, *What a hoot!*

When we arrived on the scene, a woman stood on the lawn, pointing to the front door of a one-story wood-framed house where smoke slowly drifted out. We had responded to a trash container fire, all right. But there had been some incomplete communication. The occupant didn't tell the dispatcher that the trash container was in the kitchen. I'm sure when she called in the alarm the fire smoldered in the trash container. In the time between alarm notification and scene arrival, however, the fire had climbed up the kitchen wall covered with green plastic tile. The burning petroleum-based tile spread acrid black smoke throughout the house.

The lieutenant, driver, and I still thought trash fire. As I stepped down from the tailboard, the lieutenant in a calm manner said, "Jim, bring the hand pump." We went in through the front door and then entered the kitchen immediately to our left. The fire traveled up the wall, engulfing kitchen cabinets.

The lieutenant turned to me, and in his slow, calm drawl said, "Well, Jim, maybe you should get the booster line." Because of his demeanor, I never forgot that.

The one-inch-inside-diameter booster line had a thick red rubber coating. The line rolled up on a hose reel at the back of the pumper in front of the tailboard. As I began pulling the booster line from its reel, the driver put the pump in gear. That switched the motor to the pumping function and charged the hose line with water from the truck's tank.

The lieutenant stood by the front door. As I approached, he got down on his hands and knees. I followed suit, and we crawled into the dark structure. I felt my heart rate increase and the adrenaline rush from thoughts of danger. The lieutenant didn't take the nozzle from my hands. Instead, he placed his left arm around my back and positioned himself slightly behind me and to my right. The blazing cabinets provided enough light that I saw the outline of the lieutenant's right hand. "Hit the fire right there!" We extinguished the fire in an instant, but the smoke remained.

Seasoned firefighters were slowly transitioning to the use of breathing apparatus as they began shedding the macho image in favor of good health. Because of this fire's size, the lieutenant made a decision to knock it down quickly so that we wouldn't have to call for additional help. That would've been a bigger violation of the "Dude Code." Instead of taking the time to don air tanks with masks, we utilized the controlled slow-and-shallow breathing technique. As a result, smoke entered our sinuses and lungs, and our sinuses drained profusely. Long strings of black snot hung down to my neck. I cleared my nasal passages by closing off each nostril and blowing black snot rockets to the ground. I coughed up some of the black poison and hacked it out, but no doubt some remained in my lungs. I learned later that researchers can easily determine the amount of toxins in a body from one exposure, but the cumulative effect of many exposures cannot be quantified. However, enough research has been conducted that firefighters' cancers are now presumed job-related.

I noticed one more thing during my first firefighting operation. My heartbeats and breathing respirations seemed a little quicker than my seasoned officer's.

The driver brought a ventilation fan, set it in the front door, and started ventilating smoke. We finished debris cleanup, took the appropriate information from the occupant for a fire report, and returned to the station. We cleaned our equipment and placed the pumper back in service.

My training had worked, but that lieutenant impressed me. A crew cut crowned his lanky six-foot frame complete with long legs. His friendly demeanor with a constant smile made everyone around him comfortable. In everyday life or at an emergency scene, he was the coolest and calmest person I'd ever met.

Several other things occurred during that first alarm. The lieutenant let me extinguish the fire using a minimal amount of water. He calmed me down in a hostile environment. He witnessed my baptism by smoke and conveyed the same to others. I passed the real test for the old heads because my lieutenant confirmed that I hung in there without an air tank.

I asked, "When do we wear air tanks?"

The answer came quickly. "When you fight a real fire."

Firefighters who didn't hang in during a tough situation received nicknames like "door holder" for the real firefighters who crossed danger's threshold.

Firefighters strive for distinction. That lieutenant's natural calm behavior became his distinction. That day he became my hero lieutenant, due mainly to his demeanor. That first alarm began my professional quest to pay attention. I began calmly applying what I learned to the question of how to more efficiently and effectively handle emergencies.

That night I showered, ate dinner, watched a little television, and after Bo sharpened my knife, went to bed about 10:30 p.m. I lay in bed and got ready for a legitimate sleeping session. Although no more alarms occurred that night, I couldn't sleep well because of recalling the day's activities and anticipating another potential alarm. I kept thinking, *Make sure you dress quickly. Slide the pole the way you were taught. Don your protective gear. Step up on the tailboard, and click the safety belt shut. Listen for your officer's instructions at an emergency scene. Why are other firefighters peacefully snoring? Who's the guy in the far corner of the bunkroom that sounds like a truck without a muffler? Unbelievable!*

6

POLE-POSITION DOMINATION

Firefighters use four-inch-diameter steel poles when traveling from upper to lower station floors. Older brass poles have two disadvantages. Keeping them beautiful requires constant polishing. Brass poles also build up friction more quickly than steel, so firefighters' hands get burned when sliding. Firefighters either slide down brass poles with cleaning rags in their hands or wrap their elbows around the poles if they wear long-sleeved shirts. Steel poles provide less friction and require no maintenance. In fact, firefighters' belt buckles help polish steel poles while sliding. The polished portion of the steel poles begins about the three-foot level above the top floor and goes to about the three-foot level above the bottom floor, depending of course on the length of firefighters' legs. Poles quicken the "turnout" time as part of the total response time.

Turnout time starts when an alarm sounds and ends when a firefighter is on a truck, ready for responding. Bodies react with an increased heart rate in anticipation of the unknown, because every alarm leads to a different scene. Heart rates also increase with physical activity. Firefighters sublimate these physiological reactions for a safe turnout sequence.

During the day, if an alarm sounds, firefighters hustle to their vehicles and dress in their protective gear. The gear includes a sturdy coat, rubber gloves, a helmet, and rubber boots. The boot tops fold down to the calf tops, for comfortable walking. Upon arrival at a fire scene, firefighters grab the boot tops and quickly pull them up.

At night, station speakers click on, lights automatically turn on, and electronic alarm tones sound. Fire coats, gloves, and helmets lie on fire trucks, ready for donning.

Bunker gear sits next to the bunks so that firefighters can dress quickly. The bunker gear includes a pair of shorter fire boots that come up to the calves. Each side of the boots has a molded loop, like on cowboy boots. Bunker pants have linings and the outer layers are made from the same material as fire coats. The bunker pant legs fit over bunker boots and push down in an accordion fashion. Boot tops are exposed for easy access. The top part of the bunker pants has flexible suspenders attached that drape over the outer sides of the pants and boots.

When an alarm sounds, firefighters swing both legs over the side of their bunk and place their feet in the boots. After they stand, the bunker pant tops pull up to the waist, and a snap hook clicks shut in a clasp. Finally, in one sweeping motion, the suspenders are placed on shoulders. Firefighters then slide down a pole attached to the ceiling of the second story and extending down through a large hole in the second-story floor to ground level.

During turnout training, rookies lay on their bunks, and when trainers said, "Go," the exercise began. The exercise ended when rookies slid a pole, donned their remaining protective gear, and stepped up on a pumper tailboard, ready to respond. The timed exercise sometimes needed repeating, so rookies climbed the stairs, lay down on their bunks, and started over.

The need for repeating an exercise depended on several factors. Those included how well and how quickly a rookie performed the exercise. Another factor included trainers' motives. More often than not, the motive included teasing or initiating. The number of on-duty personnel who lined up for encouragement gave a clue that an initiation process had begun. Words of encouragement included phrases like "Hurry up, come on, man," "People are trapped," "Your team's waiting downstairs!" "All right, rookie, start over," or "That seemed okay, but let's do it again."

The turnout time sequence needed extra practice because at night turnout took longer than in the day. All those exercises had a purpose, and that purpose guaranteed proficiency at responding from a nighttime "readiness to serve posture."

I later learned that turnout was part of a series of events called "total response time." The series includes several timed events:

1. Time from noticing an emergency to calling 911;
2. Time from 911 dispatch notification to dispatchers alarming fire stations;
3. Time from station's alert to turnout time on a fire vehicle;
4. Time from a fire vehicle moving to arriving at an emergency scene, called travel time.

Travel time is the only variable that can be shortened by the number and location of fire stations. More stations strategically placed shorten average travel times.

Firefighters access a sliding pole by first grabbing it with both hands above the head, thereby avoiding a slight free-fall before legs wrap around the pole. Firefighters mount a pole by gently leaning against it below the collarbone. The shin and top of a foot press against a pole's front side, while the calf and heel of the other foot clamp around a pole's back side. After mounting a pole, speed and braking become a concern. Squeezing legs together provides the best down-the-pole slowing.

When some rookies begin, it all appears in slow motion. They bring their feet to the edge of a giant round abyss, then reach up and grab a pole with their dominant hand, followed by their less dominant hand. They slowly lean into a pole while keeping both feet on terra firma. Ever so slowly, they put one foot forward next to a pole. Their other foot and leg then clamp around the back side of a pole. Their hands and legs clamp so tightly they look like wide-eyed monkeys frozen on tree limbs. They understand the braking part now. With encouragement, they slightly loosen their death grips and slide about one foot at a time. That jerking motion and squeaking sound continue all the way down.

The speed part of the maneuver is necessary for obvious reasons. Firefighters descend quickly and step away from the bottom to avoid being crushed by the next firefighter sliding down. This is particularly important at night, when firefighters aren't completely conscious yet. I witnessed my first workplace accident (mistake) during this time; it's why the first station I helped design had no poles. The kitchen area, office area, and classroom sat half belowground. That meant the second story, which contained the bunkroom and restrooms, only needed half the number of wide-tread steps to the ground floor. That station remains in service today on South Broadway across the street from the fire museum and fallen firefighter memorial.

In my rookie year, I had the same fascination with the pole as with the water-and-oil-sealed floor. One day, an alarm sounded after I'd washed my hands, so I couldn't casually dry them. When I mounted the pole, my wet hands caused a slight slippage. That lasted briefly but also left a damp spot on the pole for the next firefighter. I never did that again.

My pole obsession didn't end. I looked for ways to improve maneuvers or at least make the task humorous. We always looked for competitive activity. Little feats of meaningless excellence sometimes hastened team acceptance.

One such challenge for me became dominance at sliding a pole. After much in-service training, I free-fell down a pole while simultaneously wrapping my legs and grasping my hands around it. After free-falling almost two feet, I clamped my legs and hands together so that I stopped at the last second before reaching the floor. Legs held the secret because I easily slid a pole without both of my hands. I also slid a pole in a twirling fashion with only one hand.

My final attempt at pole-position domination came one day when a fellow firefighter and I contemplated the possibility of sliding a pole upside down.

"Do you think you can do it?"

"I don't know, but let's give it a try."

I did and still do have a desire for continued well-being, and that's why we didn't start on the upper floor. The attempt began by rounding up a couple of the biggest horses. The "horse" designation applied to firefighters of great size and physical strength. Those guys could hit someone on the top of their head and break the arches in their feet. We approached the two biggest horses for their assistance.

I still remember their immediate response. "We gotta see this."

First, I stood upside down on my hands on the lower-level floor with my legs wrapped around the pole. The two horses, there to witness my apocalyptic attempt, hoisted me up off the floor. They slowly let go but continued "spotting" me. Thank goodness, because it didn't work. They lowered me safely to the ground and waited for a second attempt.

After the blood returned in my lower extremities, we surmised that my hands hadn't provided enough gripping strength. For the second attempt, we began the same way, only this time my elbows remained next to my body with hands and forearms clutching the pole next to my chest. That yielded better results, so the horses pushed me as high as they could and loosened their grip but continued spotting me. With all my strength, I awkwardly made it down the pole about two inches.

A tiny "No" came out of my mouth.

They safely lowered me to the floor because a third attempt seemed inevitable. I sat still for a few moments while blood again drained back into my lower body. I also made sure that I hadn't popped a blood vessel in my peanut-sized brain. Normally I would have analyzed the situation and prepared for another try, but as with the pilot training, I knew when to walk away.

When a third attempt didn't happen, three comments followed.

The first horse said, "Wimp."

To that, I responded, "You try it."

The second horse said, "You do know that I just saved your life."

"Thank you."

The final comment came from out of earshot of the others when my original collaborator softly said, "At least you tried. That's more than they did."

7

Picking Up Horses

I sought distinguishing feats that involved balance or flexibility. The origin of this ambition could be traced back to my only high school sport: gymnastics. I competed in floor exercise and tumbling. Two main differences separate the gymnastics I practiced in the early 1960s from now. Participants today are far superior athletes, and the routines of tumbling and floor exercise are combined and performed on padded floors. We performed our floor exercise routines on the hardwood floors of a basketball half-court. I didn't excel at floor exercise, except for a few strength and flexibility exercises.

Tumbling began with a running start. Upon reaching padded mats, gymnasts did a roundoff back handspring, which provided momentum for a series of backward handsprings and backflips. A forward routine followed that, going in the opposite direction. Although successful in citywide competitions, I never did better than fifth place in state competitions.

Except for football and basketball, no specialized high school coaching existed in the 1960s. Even football and basketball coaches taught boys' gym classes. The driver education teacher taught gymnastics. That's the equivalent of fire training being taught by a finance director, although I've known a couple of finance directors who thought they knew everything about firefighting.

The gymnastics coach excelled as a driver education teacher, but when it came to gymnastics, he didn't know his butt from two hot rocks. He showed us a poster on a wall that had a series of pictures demonstrating each maneuver. We practiced, sometimes with a spotter and sometimes without one. When coming off a high backflip we "stuck" a landing straight-legged, rather than flexing our knees and then standing up, because that's what the pictures demonstrated.

Once during a competition, I nailed the landing but hyperextended my right knee. A loud pop echoed in the quiet gymnasium, followed by some sympathetic oohs and gasps from the audience. I hobbled over to the bench, and that ended my season. The next year I competed again and received the same injury, which ended my competition. After that, we learned of my torn anterior cruciate ligament. The swelling occurred as a result of synovial fluid leaking out from a sac surrounding the knee joint.

When the same injury happened the third time, years later, the doctor drained the fluid by inserting a needle into the knee joint. The needle resembled a javelin. The fourth injury resulted in the same treatment. The fifth injury occurred years later. That time, instead of fluid, blood came out, so the time arrived for an anterior cruciate reconstruction. I will finish the story of that barbaric practice later. That's when I understood, however, what "practicing" medicine meant. The driver education teacher received extra pay for after-school coaching while some of us received lifelong injuries.

The positive and long-lasting benefits of gymnastics included accomplishing backflips, back handsprings, and handstands, walking on my hands, and various flexibility exercises. Demonstration of those insignificant talents always came at the appropriate time. When a fellow firefighter pulled off some feat, I'd say, "Oh yeah, try this," and do a standing backflip.

In the kitchen, I stood sideways to the cabinets, squatted down, and jumped thirty-six inches to the countertop. Although not easy, it wasn't that hard if you jumped at an angle to the countertop while tucking your legs and landing on the one-foot-wide space that extended beyond the upper cabinets.

I displayed my talent one day when we responded to a downtown alarm near Douglas and Topeka. After the alarm, our pumper and crew remained on the scene. Several kids gathered around while I talked to Captain Kendal Seaman. The captain struck up a conversation with the youngsters when one of them asked, "How can I become a firefighter?"

I knew what he wanted when the captain looked at me. "Show them, Jim."

I took off my fire coat and did a back handspring in the middle of the street with my fire boots on. The captain turned to the wide-eyed youngsters. "That's what it takes to become a firefighter."

After a few moments of silence, the youngsters glanced back and forth from the captain to me. I cracked a smile. That's when one of them said, "No way."

The captain then gave the standard response. "Listen to your parents, stay in school, and obey the law."

My nonprofessional achievements needed a strength exercise. My only above-average strength was in my legs. One day the horses bragged about an off-duty weight-lifting achievement when one of them turned to me. "There's something you can't do."

I quickly shot back, "No, but I'll bet you a Coke I can pick you up."

The details needed clarifying because, believe it or not, some men attempted trickery. After the usual clarification, I positioned the 230-pound horse so that he stood still with feet apart. I got behind the horse and squatted down so the horse could sit on my shoulders. With some straining, I raised the horse off the ground and then quickly squatted down to let him stand while slowly backing away. Naturally, cries of foul echoed until I reminded them they had had an opportunity for clarification. Slurping sounds of a delicious soft drink grew louder once again, but I was the only one smiling.

About that time, my preparation for the probationary exam intensified as the testing date got closer.

Floor Exercise

8

BLOODY SPOT
ON THE CHICKEN THEORY

At the end of my probationary period, I passed my test, but one rookie destined for the private sector flunked his exam. One of the addresses with hydrant locations he missed, 500 South Topeka, was the address of our fire station. In addition to questions relating to the red book, the test had random addresses in our response district with two blank lines. We filled in those blank lines with the location of the two closest fire hydrants to those addresses. We needed to know two hydrant locations in the event one failed or a secondary water supply became necessary. We memorized all the streets and fire hydrant locations in our response district.

A long time ago someone figured out that when an alarm sounded, and a dispatcher announced the kind of alarm and address, it would be a good idea if firefighters knew the route to that address. Identifying the two closest hydrant locations confirmed a firefighter knew both the address and water supply locations.

Over the first one and a half years in the fire service, I responded to different types of alarms. Occasionally a fire spread to an attic or crawl space, and the need existed for a medium-built, flexible firefighter who could wiggle through an access hole, receive a hose line, and extinguish the fire. On those few occasions, I benefited the team and gained valuable knowledge on fire travel. I always paid attention.

I paid attention to daily station life as well, and the interactions between ranks. Individual firefighters had unique personalities. Some officers, like the hero lieutenant, received more respect than others, and some younger firefighters moved up the ranks more quickly. Some firefighters had better verbal volleyball skills and better reactions to teasing. All successful firefighters had good communication and social skills that adapted easily to different situations.

Teasing happened during bunker turnout training to test a rookie's sensitivity level. Another of the favorites occurred when someone challenged a rookie firefighter. "Can you lean your head back, look at the ceiling with a coin on your forehead, and balance a large funnel down the front part of your pants?"

"Of course."

"Here's the hard part. Can you then tilt your head forward and catch a coin in that funnel? Here, we will demonstrate the challenge for you."

Naturally, a dry run demonstrated by someone else showed the ease of task accomplishment. While a hapless rookie concentrated on dropping a coin in the funnel, another firefighter poured a glass of water down the funnel, leaving a rookie looking like he wet himself.

If a rookie got mad or began whining, other teasing episodes usually followed. Conversely, if a rookie didn't react or better yet laughed with the group, usually nothing else happened. Paying attention to those events and consequences resulted in what I called the "bloody spot on the chicken theory."

Years later I explained that theory to rookies. "If a chicken somehow gets a bloody spot, other chickens peck at it, sometimes pecking the chicken to death." I told the rookies, "Don't show your bloody spot."

I also told them what they didn't have to tolerate. That included anything involving a protected status such as race or gender. I shared how none of my previous jobs carried the same job satisfaction as a career in the fire service. I always said, "I eagerly anticipated every workday and the first day after vacation. I asked about what I missed along with descriptions of fires and any medical calls." I tried conveying my job satisfaction and closed by telling rookies that reputations are established early in careers, so they needed to study diligently and perform all tasks to the best of their abilities. I also suggested they should ignore complainers and pay attention to role models who enjoyed their work and concentrated on safety.

Not long after the end of my probationary period I began paying attention to firefighting strategy and supporting tactics. I learned that different types of fires required different strategies and tactics. My first large field firefight occurred near Thirty-First Street South and

Meridian. Several grass fires occurred that day along with brisk winds. Our pumper, commanded by my hero lieutenant, responded along with others to a large field fire.

Upon arrival, we saw four-foot-high flames spreading rapidly because of the quartering wind from our left side. My lieutenant and I began making our way to an already-burned portion of the field. We always attacked an unconfined field fire from an already-burned side. That prevented the enemy from surrounding and attacking us. It was just the opposite from attacking a structure fire, where we got ahead of the confined enemy and pushed it back to the point of origin for extinguishment. That kept us from pushing flames throughout a structure, thereby causing more damage or potentially harming other firefighters attacking from the opposite direction.

While we walked across the field toward the burned area, the driver positioned the truck so we could access the booster line. The wind shifted and started pushing fire toward us. As the fire rapidly picked up speed, it became obvious that we couldn't make it to the burned area. My lieutenant stopped, turned to me, and in that same calm drawl said, "Well, Jim, maybe we should retreat."

Both he and I did an about-face and proceeded back toward the street and our pumper. The lieutenant began with a fast walk, as did I. Occasionally we glanced over our shoulders and quickened our pace. My inseam measured thirty-one inches. My hero lieutenant's inseam measured about thirty-six. He never broke into a run. From the front, he looked like that long-legged character in the "Keep on truckin'" stickers. While he loped, I ran at a quick pace. Later the driver described the retreat as "Mutt and Jeff hauling butt." We made it to the pumper and then performed our attack with a booster line from a burned area. Paying attention reinforced the "remain calm" lesson as well as the one about attacking from an already-burned side.

Having now passed my rookie test, I began considering my goal of a college education. Firefighters exchanged shifts with each other for reasons like hunting, fishing, extended vacations, and many other pursuits. Firefighters kept track of the exchange time and paid those hours back to the person who worked for them. We even exchanged partial shifts until the hours amounted to twenty-four, and the return paid back in one twenty-four-hour shift.

With that in mind, I started planning for my exchange of time when college attendance fell on duty days. I discussed this with my captain, who sent the request up the organizational ladder with his support. I don't know how many rungs up the ladder my request went, but I know the answer that came back: no.

Captain Seaman explained that because of the need for two or three hours twice per week, record keeping would be too cumbersome. I asked if we could keep track of the process ourselves. The reply came quickly. "Too much of a hassle for a station captain to enter into a logbook." Even though he disagreed with a decision made above his level, he loyally supported that decision. A few years passed by before I understood his loyalty.

I tried making out schedules of class attendance with the possibility of missing some classes. None of those ideas seemed acceptable. Not one to show my bloody spot, I started considering other options.

9

PUBLIC SERVANT RIVALRY

While discussing my exchange-of-time issue with a couple of police officer friends, they told me that police department shift work provided shifts compatible with classes. Funding also existed in the form of the LEEAP: Law Enforcement Educational Assistance Program. That intrigued me because education seemed valuable at all levels in the police department. I wrestled with the thought of leaving the fire department. City management made the decision easier because they changed the twenty-four-hour shifts to rotating ten- and fourteen-hour shifts when the workweek hours were reduced to fifty-six. The ten-hour days went from 8:00 a.m. until 6:00 p.m. The fourteen-hour shift went from 6:00 p.m. until 8:00 a.m.

At that time, police officers and firefighters had parity. Parity included pay and benefits, including retirement plans. That parity in pay and benefits let me transfer to the police department with no loss in retirement credit time served. The police department, like the fire department, actively recruited. I told Captain Seaman about my decision, and he said he understood because his children wanted a college education as well. I told him I would miss the fire department and appreciated everything he had done for me. He told me if things didn't work out, he would recommend my transfer back to the fire department. After background and fingerprinting checks, I soon found myself in rookie school again.

An unused school at the corner of Central and Waco housed the training classes. We had the three-story brick building to ourselves, except for some storage areas.

The study material and practical training fascinated me. Police training required qualifying on the firing range with my department-issued .38 caliber Smith & Wesson. I remember the range master qualifying by firing his weapon upside down, pulling the trigger with his little finger. That seemed cool, but I wondered what went through his mind when he first tried that. I never tried it because someone else had already perfected it. As in the fire department, the police department had members who performed distinguishing acts.

Another fascinating part of police training included traffic accident investigation. That included measuring the length of skid marks left by tires when the rear wheels locked. Before antilock braking systems, when someone slammed on their brakes, the rear wheels locked and left black tire marks on the pavement. The length of marks helped determine the speed of a vehicle before impact.

During one of our training modules, the training officer had one of the rookies drive a patrol car, speed up, and slam on the brakes so we could take our measurements. In the first attempt, the driver didn't apply the brakes hard enough to lock the wheels. In the second attempt, he didn't accelerate enough and left only a teeny squeak and no measurable mark.

The training officer readily let me try. I climbed into the patrol car, put the accelerator to the floor, and kept it there. As I approached the group, they all began stepping back to the curb. When almost even with the group, I stomped on the brake pedal, and the rear end of the vehicle drifted off slightly from a straight path. We had enough black tire marks for our measurements. I climbed out of the vehicle. "Will that be sufficient?"

The training officer tilted his head slightly to one side. "Oh, that's right," he smirked. "You came from the fire department!"

Over the years I found a mostly cordial relationship between firefighters and police officers. Firefighters used nicknames such as "gumshoe" and "donut eater" for police officers. Police officers used names such as "water squirter" and "hose jockey." The friendly banter sometimes progressed to a more detailed description of one's worth in society. For example, firefighters stated that police officers only gathered reports because they arrived after an incident occurred. Police officers stumbled upon emergencies still in progress en route to a donut sale, whereas firefighters responded to fires and medical calls that still needed immediate attention.

Police officers answered with "All you hose jockeys do is sleep until you get hungry and eat until you get sleepy."

My favorite insult came from a friend in Florida who told the story about the police and fire recruitment processes. After initial testing, candidates found themselves in a large hole with a ladder. Smart applicants climbed out and became firefighters. Applicants who remained in the hole became police officers.

I enjoyed the remainder of my police training, and later as class president, I gave the commencement address. Attendees included all the top brass. That was late 1968, and we were only a couple of years past the Miranda decision. My comments focused on the challenges facing law enforcement, including the recent Miranda requirement. I asserted that we could overcome those perceived barriers by working harder and smarter.

My brief career as a police officer allows only one worthwhile story. A call came over the car radio of a stabbing in a bar on North Broadway. That bar was a known hangout for a group of people who worked in a nearby slaughterhouse. They routinely carried knives and knew how to use them. When I arrived on scene, blood had pooled on the floor and the victim was gone. Since a victim didn't need treatment, I tried gathering information about what had happened but received no cooperation. And some not-so-friendly looks.

Then the vibe changed. Some looked away, and one person even had a slight smile. Either they finally noticed my badge and uniform, or they had heard about my reputation for having a bad temper. While considering the third option of my reputation for never losing a fight (except for one draw with Pee Wee), I heard a slight noise behind me. I turned around, and there in the doorway stood the tallest police officer I'd ever seen. He smiled broadly. The lanky officer asked, "Is everything okay?"

"It is now."

I completed my gathering of information thanks to his influence. That police officer later climbed to the second-highest rung on the organizational ladder.

The fight with Pee Wee happened one evening by North High School not long after graduation. I stood about five six. Pee Wee was an inch shorter. I don't even remember why the fight started, but I do remember how. We circled, facing each other in preparation for a boxing match. I threw the first few swings and missed because I didn't know how to box. But somebody had taught Pee Wee how to box because the next thing I knew my nose bled and I saw stars. Boxing wasn't working, so I took Pee Wee to the ground and got a couple of punches in when he said, "Let's box."

"No, thanks. But I am willing to call it a draw."

Pee Wee said okay, and we went our separate ways.

Years later I ran into him in a bar on South Seneca, and he wore a military uniform. He hadn't gained much height, but from the waist up he looked like an upside-down pyramid. We had a friendly conversation, thank goodness, because I know how that tussle would have turned out.

Six months into my police career a couple of things changed in the fire department. The new shift schedule had several ten-hour days in a row with a couple of days off, followed by several fourteen-hour nights. Continual switching from day to night shifts was difficult on families and days-off employment. Opposition to the ten- and fourteen-hour schedules grew, and turnover increased. That high turnover rate caused the pending change back to twenty-four-hour shifts beginning January 1.

The fire department's chief training officer and Captain Seaman confirmed that the policy on trading time for college attendance had also changed. One story claimed no change occurred, rather "clarification," and that trading time for college was always allowed. My former request had only made it two rungs up the ladder. As a result, when I moved up that ladder, I developed an open-door policy and ordered zero tolerance for blocked communication. The pending change back to twenty-four-hour shifts and clarification on rules regarding trading time for college led me back to the fire department. I came back with a few months left on the ten- and fourteen-hour shift schedule because of vacancies. Captain Seaman and the chief training officer favorably recommended my transfer back to the fire department.

A philosopher once said, "Those who have experienced both sides of an issue are best able to judge." I can state unequivocally that police officers have a more thankless job. For almost every incident firefighters respond to, people want them there. Whereas, when police officers respond, one or more people don't appreciate their presence. From my point of view, being a police officer is a noble calling that sometimes requires searching for job satisfaction.

An unforgettable event occurred while I was still a police officer. The evening news reported the story of a large fire in progress at a downtown car dealership. The roof of the building had collapsed, and four fire personnel had gone missing. I walked outside, climbed onto the roof of my one-story apartment building, and saw a large orange glow in the sky from south Wichita. Shortly after that, an announcement came that the fire chief and three other fire personnel had died in a roof collapse. I hadn't met any of the firefighters and only knew the fire chief as the department head in charge when I first joined the department. I didn't understand that tragedy for years until the introduction of incident command, which I will explain later.

10

BULIMIA

Upon transferring back to the fire department, I performed an act of contrition. That act included time on probation and retaking my rookie test, but I felt gratefully reemployed in an enjoyable career. Administration assigned me to District 1, Station 1. The rookie test provided no challenge, except for memorizing hydrant locations. I had attended schools and lived in the western and northern parts of the city, so street locations presented no challenge.

I memorized hydrant locations with rhyming verses. I recall only one mnemonic device. It went something like this: "Up your gee gee, down your spine. Central, Pine, two, three, nine." That verse meant hydrants were on the east/west streets of Second, Third, Central, Pine, and Ninth Streets. I don't remember what north/south street the verse applied to because each street had different hydrant locations. The verses apparently helped, because I passed my second rookie test.

Fire Station No. 1 replicated Station 2, but also housed a vehicle maintenance facility and crowded offices for the top brass. Both stations had a watchman's booth located in the center of the bay floor. The booth, elevated from the bay floor, had steps leading up to the room containing an office chair and desktop. Glass encapsulated the front-facing view and both sides, similar to an air traffic control tower. We staffed the watchman's booth from 8:00 a.m. to 8:00 p.m. The watchman kept his eyes on the entire area because anyone could enter.

The watchman had a microphone and gave signals over the station speakers. For instance, if women or children entered downstairs, the watchman announced, "Signal five, thirty-three." If women or children headed upstairs, the watchman announced, "Signal five, sixty-six." There were other signals for various situations.

The Station 1 watchman always looked out for the fire chief, who parked in the last position of a bay in front of an overhead back door. If the chief announced his arrival at Station 1 over the radio system, the watchman hurried down the steps and opened the overhead back door. He closed the door after the chief drove in and returned to the booth. When the chief left, the entire process reversed, but without a car radio announcement, the watchman paid attention. The chief left precisely at 5:00 p.m., but sometimes the only warning a watchman received came from the sound of the chief's footsteps or his car door shutting. A pumper parked in front of the fire chief's car, and a district chief vehicle parked in front of the pumper. When the pumper and district chief vehicle parked in the station, the fire chief came and went via the rear bay door.

One day, as I sat on watch, memorizing my hydrant verses, I heard the sound of a car door shutting. I looked down from the watchman's booth and saw the fire chief sitting in his vehicle. His appointment as fire chief filled the vacancy created by the previous chief's death. Like the previous chief, he had a career reputation as a fierce interior-attack firefighter and officer. The district chief's car and pumper had left the station, and the front bay door remained open. I waited for the chief to start his vehicle and drive through the empty bay and out the front door. I glanced back at him. He sat still, looking up at me.

The visual presence of that man was intimidating. His height exceeded six feet, and he had white hair and bushy white eyebrows, the total embodiment of command presence. The mere narrowing of his eyelids meant something needed a quick response. He hadn't even finished the narrowing part when I hustled down the stairs and opened the back door. Just as I accomplished that task, he started his car and drove through the open bay and out the front door, as I originally thought he would. About halfway through his slow journey exiting the station, his reflection with a wry smile appeared in his side view mirror. In case he circled the block and came back for something, I didn't close the rear door.

By the end of 1969, I had over two years' seniority. Other firefighters and I became more involved with union activity because of the ten- and fourteen-hour shifts. That shift schedule demoralized department personnel. In retrospect, the shifts didn't seem like a good move on management's part. City management's decisions, especially implementing those work hours, only strengthened the union, increasing the divide between labor and management and contributing to turnover.

As a management right, transfers and station assignments occurred at the sole discretion of management. My first transfer sent me to an outlying station. That newer station, like most outlying facilities, housed a pumper and an aerial ladder. Two bays, which separated the living quarters, had both front and rear overhead doors. One side adjoining the bay included the bunkroom, lockers, showers, and restroom facilities. The other side included an office and a combination kitchen, dining, and television area. All but two of the outlying stations had one level, so my pole-position domination days ended.

My new station life seemed far less hectic. The smaller station had fewer personnel and received fewer alarms. I focused on little things that fascinated me, like sliding mayonnaise jars. Our dining table, about ten feet long and four feet wide, had laminate covering on the top and edges. One day, I cleaned the dining table with a wet dishcloth and retrieved a dry cloth for removing the water droplets. Another firefighter took a jar of mayonnaise out of the refrigerator, walked over to the table, set the jar down, and slid it to the middle of the table. The wet tabletop provided little friction. The mayonnaise jar began its quick slide and seemed hell-bent for falling off the other end.

I stood helplessly off to the side with a dry towel in my hand. The firefighter took hold of the table and gave it a hard shove in the direction of jar travel. That one move stopped the jar two feet short of its impending disaster. That's one of many quick-thinking examples I've observed. That type of quick thinking routinely occurred on all rescue operations.

One captain at that station had a lot of time on the job. After every meal, he excused himself and went over to the other side of the station. "What's going on?" I asked my companions.

Someone said, "The captain's bulimic." That didn't make sense because he didn't fit the stereotype. Further inquiry revealed a formal pattern. The captain went over to the restroom after every meal. He ran water in his hand, started slurping water into his mouth, began gagging, headed for an open stall, and vomited. I don't recall whether the captain said something or did something, or if a dare surfaced, but someone took action.

Before one of our meals, a member of our crew went over to the toilet stalls, locked all the doors, and slid out through the bottom. We all gathered for our family meal. Right on time, the captain excused himself from the table, crossed the bay area, and entered the realm of restroom weight control. We heard some awful sounds through two sets of doors and the distance of both bays. Some time passed before the captain came back. By then we finished kitchen cleanup and sat watching television with feigned attention. I don't remember any conversation because what could he say, "Who interrupted my secret disgusting regimen?"

Daytime drinking was one of many problems with the ten- and fourteen-hour shifts. Some members reported for the 6:00 p.m. shift with alcohol still in their system. The drinking before duty became bad enough that word came down from the top rung of the ladder to cease.

The captain admitted that he drank, so I instituted a bogus but humorous breath check when we began the 6:00 p.m. shift. For some reason, the captain used mouthwash at the beginning of an evening shift before my breath checks. I started with the captain—and immediately ended. Everyone including the captain enjoyed the ritual, or so I thought. Due diligence would have revealed that the captain and someone near the top rung of the ladder had been friends for many years.

Consequently, one shift I settled into my new environment and the next found me in Station 1 for a short period. Not long afterward, another transfer sent me to Fire Station No. 10, in the northeast section of Wichita, a far less affluent section of the city. Station 10, located at the corner of Seventeenth and Grove, had earlier been part of the city's racial conflicts, which were similar to what had occurred in other cities nationwide in that era. The pumper still had a small bullet hole in the front next to the siren from a shot fired while it was at a house fire. Until the social unrest and rioting quieted down, police squads escorted fire vehicles to all fires in the northeast section of Wichita. That made several firefighters carry concealed weapons in their fire coats. Those times of uncertainty created fear of the unknown. Besides aggression toward firefighters, the looting and burning of neighbors' businesses was most puzzling. By the time I arrived at Station 10, however, good community relations had been restored.

The fire department had integrated ten years earlier, before 1960. The integration process made most members unhappy, including black firefighters, partly because they were guaranteed promotions in a segregated station. District chief promotions, however, couldn't be attained until integration because those promotions came from one of the three unintegrated headquarter stations.

Race riots and war protests occurred nationwide in the late 1960s, with war protests continuing into the early 1970s. The same anti-war sentiment was expressed at Wichita State University in the form of protests. Because of my father's military service and my paramilitary status as a firefighter, I found myself at odds with the anti-war folk. The divide didn't result from their opposition to the war, but rather from their vilification of military personnel. That divide cemented when the Reserve Officers' Training Corp (ROTC) building had a fire of suspicious origin. ROTC members seemed unwelcome on campus and sometimes were the objects of ridicule. I noticed a couple of hippies pointing at me one day. One of them glanced more closely at my shoulder patch and declared, "Oh, he's a fireman."

"No. I'm a firefighter. Firemen shovel coal into boilers on trains." After that day, I wore my uniform at every opportunity.

Wichita, only two years removed from the racial conflict, had endured a mandatory curfew from 10:00 p.m. until 6:00 a.m. The fire department integrated before the social unrest of 1968, so no departmental issues remained, only individuals who harbored issues. The community and fire department relationship healed fairly quickly because of the services we offered, which everyone appreciated. Police officers, who didn't share the same community relations, viewed Station 10 as an oasis for report writing and friendly surroundings.

Station 10 housed only one pumper, which annually responded to more alarms than any pumper in the city. Assignment there sometimes signaled a firefighter's banishment. Union participation still had some stigma attached from years before that was never fully forgotten. In the 1950s, the city made firefighters give up their union charter, and the us-against-them mentality still existed. I'm not saying my union participation became the reason for my transfers, but I'm sure it didn't help. For whatever reason, administration transferred me to a facility that gave me a lot of firefighting experience and close proximity to the university. Thank you so much.

The spring of 1970 found me back in college with more firsthand awareness of social issues like poverty and racism. It took my paying attention to some of the college literature I read and focusing on two people I admired, however, to change some of my behavior, such as laughing at racial slurs. Occasionally I threw in an offensive word of my own to demonstrate my "one of the boys" social bond. High school was where I first heard those words. Later, there will be more on this and two people I admired who happened to be minorities.

Years later, I used the changes brought about in my own life to effect changes in subordinates' use of racial slurs. I knew that people's minds wouldn't change, but their behavior on the job was changeable. How employees talked on their own time was none of my business, but their language on the job put the employer at risk. During my administrative tenure in another city, I recommended discipline for two employees because of their language. The men had used inappropriate language while on duty in my presence. I ordered one of them, an officer, to read a story by Flannery O'Connor, the title of which contained the slur he had used, and write a book report. The word must've gotten out because it didn't happen again.

11

BAD MANAGEMENT, STRONG UNION

I served at Station 10 from 1970 to 1977. During that time, I had another failed marriage and this time a son, Derek. I met my second wife in a bar, where she worked as a dancer. After a little over five years, our lives took different directions and we drifted apart. I spent weekend time with my daughter, Shelley, and son, Derek, and in addition my son stayed with me on some of my days off from the fire department. In the 1970s I was simultaneously a father, a firefighter, a college student, and a union activist. The union involvement began with attending meetings and progressed to the point of throwing my hat in the ring for sergeant at arms. Shortly thereafter I began developing ideas on organizational growth and success. Developing a successful organization started with the person at the top. I soon ran for union president.

I had an easy campaign because the previous president experienced some courtroom difficulties. As he explained it, when the judge announced the amount of alimony he'd owe, it exceeded his firefighter pay. He said he saw the words coming out of his mouth in slow motion. "Why, you crazy old fool." He desperately felt like grabbing hold of the sentence and pushing it back into his mouth, but it was too late. That sentence resulted in some jail time. He should have waited until after the courtroom proceedings, then exercised his free speech rights and given his opinion of the judge's decree.

Since the union wasn't a recognized collective bargaining unit for a contractual agreement, we worked through the political process. Because management didn't have to negotiate, political pressure on management was our only avenue.

We tried getting a pay increase of $100 per month, which exceeded the small percentage of pay raise allowed by wage controls. The Nixon administration imposed wage and price controls in 1971–72 in an attempt to curb inflation. Our union, the International Association of Fire Fighters (IAFF), explained that our pay raise could be compared to that of all city employees, and that would keep the total city employees' percentage below the controls. We took that proposal to the political leaders who supported the idea. City management opposed the raise because all city employees wouldn't receive the same. The turnover problem was more serious with police and fire because of all the time and money invested in recruitment and training. We succeeded politically, and police received the same raises. Management, of course, found a way that compensated other employees.

Except for the pay raises, other union goals such as reduction in workweek hours and better benefits wouldn't succeed until we achieved collective bargaining rights. By working through the political process, we finally gained formal recognition for collective bargaining. I testified at the hearing for "unit determination," that is, what ranks should be in the bargaining unit. The union wanted as many ranks as possible included, and the city wanted as few as possible. I testified that the ranks should include privates, lieutenants, and captains. We had some testimony from the ranks of private and lieutenant, but limited participation for fear of reprisal. Lieutenant Larry Thomas, a man of substance, testified on the union's behalf, and I respected his courage. I remember him stating, "I know I won't be promoted beyond lieutenant but will testify anyway." No captains testified for fear of retaliation. We succeeded in having privates and lieutenants included in the bargaining unit. Years later, captains were included as part of the bargaining unit. All designated chief officer ranks remained part of management.

State law defined the separating factors for management as their influencing ability on hiring, firing, promoting, demoting, transferring, and assigning of work. The last part, assigning, included workplace assignments. As a union representative, I always stayed out of those rights reserved for management. One of the first union seminars I attended, a John P. Redmond Symposium, concentrated exclusively on firefighter health and safety. That symposium and the following Redmond symposia led to my lifelong commitment to this important goal.

In addition to health and safety, I concentrated on wages, hours of work, and benefits. We succeeded in our first contract negotiations. The first negotiated workweek hour reduction came in the form of two twenty-four-hour shifts off per year. Later, we succeeded in negotiating two more twenty-four-hour shifts off, one for each quarter. That reduced the average fifty-six-hour workweek to fifty-three and kept the twenty-four-hour shifts.

This technical paragraph is for every firefighter who became incensed about my talk of sleeping and getting paid for it. Most jobs have set hours and shifts. If someone doesn't work for any reason, the position remains vacant, as on weekends. If firefighters worked three shifts on a forty-hour workweek and provided 24/7 protection, five people are required for one position. The two additional people cover all the weekends and other lost time due to vacations, sick leave, training, et cetera. Since most firefighters work fifty-three hours per week, only three and one-half people are needed for filling one position 24/7. That one-half, paid by firefighters working overtime, covers the lost time mentioned above. Simply stated, the additional personnel costs and benefits for a forty-hour workweek would be astronomical.

Management didn't appreciate having collective bargaining forced on them. When we negotiated for the reduced workweek hours, the city's negotiator asked, "Why don't we go to eight-hour shifts and give you a forty-hour workweek?"

He knew that would drive a wedge between the rank and file employees. He knew of the morale issues involved with the ten- and fourteen-hour shifts previously abandoned. He also knew about my quick temper because I walked out of a session earlier when he'd suggested that. I had already warned the team that that phony offer might surface again, and the city couldn't afford the additional personnel needed for that proposal.

The city's negotiator smiled as he began the meeting. "Have you given any thought to our forty-hour workweek proposal?"

I leaned across the table and looked straight into his eyes. "We accept your proposal. Would it be okay if we start Monday morning?"

Now his butt was caught in a crack because if he tried taking it back, he would open the city up to a charge of bad faith bargaining. Some stammering occurred, and he questioned whether we represented the membership. We reiterated our acceptance of his offer, and the negotiator called for a caucus. When we reconvened, the city accepted our proposal for the reduced workweek hours on twenty-four-hour shifts.

Not long afterward we had a new fire chief who worked with the union. He served as both an operations and administration deputy and always listened to new ideas and suggestions. He agreed that we needed new protective firefighting clothing but couldn't secure the funding. Politicians had the final say on the use of community development block grant funds given by the federal government to local communities. The fire chief readily let me make a presentation to the city commission. Different interest groups submitted proposals to the city commission on the allocation of those funds. I made a presentation seeking funds for the newest yellow fire coat and protective pant gear technology that provided more heat-resistant protection for all personnel. Our political efforts paid off. After a trip to Washington, DC, that clarified eligibility, our proposal received funding. That demonstrated how management and labor working together accomplished a mutual goal for firefighter safety.

Another major accomplishment of the union, for retirement benefits, didn't come through negotiations even though state law allowed that. That accomplishment allowed retirement after twenty years of service at 50 percent of the average of the highest three years of pay. I campaigned for one of the elected pension board positions with a campaign promise to secure the earlier retirement option. We handled it that way instead of through negotiations because that change affected all ranks and the system itself.

Fire department management ran their candidates, but for the first time, a young private filled an elected position on the pension board effective January 1, 1975. The pension board's actuary calculated the additional contribution necessary for the change. We also looked at the overall impact regarding the two existing plans. After all the time spent working through the process, employees voted for an increase in their contribution rate that helped fund the change. A simple change to 2.5 percent from 2 percent per year of salary instantly increased most members' retirement benefits. That brought many firefighters into the union. The actuary correctly predicted there would not be an immediate flood of retirees. While in effect those benefits stabilized turnover, the politically motivated takebacks of 1979 never considered that. Employees working side by side with different benefits and a governing attitude that lacked employee appreciation fostered more bad morale and employee turnover.

One final comment on the Wichita Police & Fire Retirement System seems in order. During the late 1970s, the state of Kansas tried taking over our system because they wanted our money. They argued that we shouldn't have an unfunded liability but should proceed on a path to full funding. Their motives notwithstanding, they were right.

I talked to Tommy Vickers, a local investment businessman, and he explained the necessity. In a retirement system, an unfunded liability occurs when an insufficient amount of money exists within the system for paying all future pension costs. Instead, some systems use pay-as-you-go funding for only a few years out. A fully funded system uses employee and employer contributions along with investment earnings that pay all future pension liabilities. The Wichita Police & Fire Retirement System shifted to a goal of full funding in twenty years. That process began in about 1976 and reached its goal in the 1990s. There will always be some fluctuations due to investment successes and setbacks. The politicians, employees, pension board, and administrators all did the right thing, unlike other communities that are in financial difficulties today.

The biggest challenge becomes resisting temptation to reduce the city's or employees' contribution rate when investment returns exceed the 100 percent funding level. The move away from 100 percent funding almost always begins with a statement like: An incorporated government will always be in business so there's no need for 100 percent funding. That makes catching up more difficult during times when investment returns slow and pushes future liabilities off onto others. That happens when political decisions are substituted for sound financial decisions. The redirected money is used for funding political policies or projects that help reelect politicians. All politicians stand for reelection.

My involvement with the union continued until I started the process of competing for a supervisory position around 1978, when the strike happened. During my union participation, I had only two disagreements with the union. First, complaining about what management received only detracted from concentrating on the union's business. Several members made statements like "Management's well paid and happy, but the firefighters have bad morale." Morale varied from shift to shift and station to station. Bad morale became evident when excessive use of sick leave occurred across the board, and people left before they could retire. We witnessed that during the ten- and fourteen-hour shift scheduling and the 1978 strike. When morale is sporadically bad, it can be traced directly to company officers, because other firefighting companies, with good officers, keep morale high.

My second disagreement with the union resulted during the strike. I knew about being belittled, ignored, and even vilified, but nobody had striking rights. The collective bargaining contract specifically prohibited striking. I used that as a selling point for collective bargaining. Some said that the strike succeeded because of a negotiated 10 percent raise over a three-year period. It's not a coincidence that continued reduction in personnel and takebacks started at the same time. How did the union think politicians would pay for those raises? Politicians through city management couldn't retaliate against individual firefighters, but they could make the department pay with personnel reductions and takebacks.

It's also not a coincidence that a major political shift occurred when takebacks began. Takebacks, such as the twenty-year retirement option regardless of age for all new hires after 1979 and the educational reimbursement incentive, became commonplace. Politicians tried making the retirement takeback retroactive, but a district court finding in favor of the union quickly stopped that action. That political effort, though, alienated all fire personnel including management because of threats against their existing benefits.

Doing away with the educational incentive seemed the dumbest of all takebacks. The idea originated internally with a bureaucrat, and politicians jumped on it. The bureaucrat, looking to gain political capital, argued that success at the college level would result in job advancement, and that in itself was incentive enough.

I found out about a personnel hearing the union requested because the takeback was mandated without any bargaining. The union's argument centered on the fact that, even though the educational incentive wasn't spelled out in the contract, axing the incentive still amounted to a loss in benefits. Even though I wasn't active in the union, I testified as an aggrieved member of the department. My argument: the purpose of education should be to teach people how to think, and we needed those schooled individuals at all levels in our organization. Besides, the amount of money mattered little to the overall budget. The personnel board agreed with my argument and ruled in the union's favor but acted only in an advisory capacity, so city management overruled the board's recommendation. That action eroded faith in the nonbinding due process system and further decreased any trust between labor and management.

The strike also caused retaliatory actions in the form of specific personnel reductions. Later, I continually battled attempts at decimating management ranks and the fire prevention division. I also rebuilt trust between the fire department and public, hence a focus on increased productivity.

The Wichita fire chief, promoted from administration deputy, knew of the failures of communication, having gone through the strike. After I completed my degree, we discussed those failures and their relation to the strike. Based on that conversation, he temporarily transferred me from operations to the training division to teach a six-week course on communications to all personnel. I included a training exercise that demonstrated competition versus collaboration. With a little trust the two teams could both come out winners, but that desire for competition guaranteed mutual self-destruction, as happened with the strike.

In addition to employee intimidation, when we examined the city's communication problems, everything centered on one phrase repeated over and over before the strike: "We don't have the money." Everyone knew additional revenue would generate the needed money. The city would have been better off saying, "We can generate more money, but we're not going to raise taxes or make other budgetary reductions. We will, however, negotiate a multi-year contract for the desired 10 percent wage increase." That's what happened anyway.

Responsible and effective union participation let me demonstrate leadership skills early in my career because the average time for the first promotion to lieutenant was ten years. The union also brought firefighter health and safety to the forefront. As I will later explain, an early transition to management, partly because of responsible union participation, allowed me to make positive changes for firefighter health and safety.

Other than the ten- and fourteen-hour scheduling debacle and contentious labor relations with the city, fire department management created a big generational chasm. It all began with the mere act of enforcing the hair code to the letter. In the 1970s hair symbolized a cultural war that began in the 1960s with those darn peace-loving hippies.

In the spring of 1964, my high school principal suspended me for an afternoon because the back of my hair touched my collar. I had no basis for appeal because I didn't have an unusually short neck. I answered their concerns by shaving my head. The only evidence of that high school revolt remains in a picture of me holding my newborn half sister, Lisa.

Twelve years later we still argued over the head and facial hair. Younger firefighters watched entertainment heroes with long hair and, with support from their girlfriends, imitated them. A harmonious balance of hair length was struck with the use of styling gel washed out the minute one went off duty. Then one officer on one shift, with a military background, made a decision based on his interpretation of the hair code and ordered a firefighter's haircut, or face suspension. The disagreement went clear to the city council, which passed a motion that abolished all head and facial hair codes for city employees.

Union participation again increased, and management lost some of its management rights. The union gained all its strength between 1971 and 1978. The increase in membership, gaining collective bargaining rights, and other successes happened because of bad management decisions. A strong union resulted from bad management. Good management and labor relations occurred when each stuck to their rights and worked together in good faith for the betterment of the organization.

With respect to firefighters striking, I encourage reading a book from 1975 by my longtime acquaintance Dennis Smith, *The Final Fire*. I met Dennis while active in the union. In 1972 he had written his memoir, *Report from Engine Co. 82*. I was preparing for a trip to Washington, DC, to research some issues at the IAFF headquarters. I contacted Dennis about the possibility of taking the train to New York City and visiting the Engine Co. 82 station. He graciously arranged for a two-day stay with the firefighters of the 82 Company. That became an eye-opening journey for a young kid from Kansas. Dennis's book told the compelling story of a firefighter in combat.

I responded with Engine 82 to a five-story apartment fire. Although firefighters extinguished a small fire on the fifth floor with only a hand pump, I watched each fire company waiting at the street level, as if they were daring the fire to grow. A ladder company would provide ventilation or rescue. A pumper company would get ahead of the fire with larger volumes of water, drive it back to its origin, and extinguish it. Another pumper company would make sure firefighters had a reliable source of water. The steely eyes of the chief officer scanned the building while he listened to the department radio. The orchestrated precision of each FDNY fire company, if the fire had grown, left my mouth hanging open, making a lasting impression. Those observations helped me understand the need for multiple fire companies, properly staffed, and the overall command function of specific operational tactics.

Firefighter station behavior in NYC, particularly the quest for humor, seemed much the same as back in Kansas. Engine Co. 82 in the South Bronx responded to so many alarms that they alternated stations with a less busy firehouse in Queens. That would extend the life of the trucks and lessen the workload on personnel. On the second day, the pumper we rode seemed worn-out and not well tuned. Just the bridge incline on the way to Queens slowed the truck to a crawl. As cars sailed past us and honked, firefighter Bob "the Beast" Beatly retrieved a shovel from storage, stood on top of the hose bed, and imitated stoking a train boiler with coal.

I commented, "Now you are a real fireman."

Bob autographed my copy of Dennis's book with the notation: "Remember the tolls."

Dennis autographed my copy: "In memory of your visit to Engine 82 with best wishes from a brother firefighter."

I later visited with Dennis when he gave the keynote address to a group of South Florida fire administrators. On the ride back to Broward County, he told me about his idea to provide a small metal tube for firefighters that they would carry in their pockets. The emergency tube could provide an additional three minutes of air. That additional three minutes might be all firefighters needed to make it to safety. Dennis shared my commitment to firefighter safety and always thought of ways to do something about it. He recalled our visit in the May 1992 issue of *Firehouse Magazine*.

Most people have heard some of the accounts of firefighters during 9/11 at the World Trade Center. Dennis tells a more personal and firsthand story in his book *Report from Ground Zero*.

12

NOT WHAT, RATHER HOW

Every generation rebels in some way and with varying intensity. Both of my children have rebelled against my failed marriages by holding their families together. Both children have spouses who augment their strengths and share the same commitment to family. My rebellion focused on having a college education. Nobody in my immediate family went beyond the ninth grade. After starting back in college, I took five years to complete my BA in education with a specialty in English and literature. After another seven and a half years, I completed my master's in urban affairs, now called public administration.

My desire for higher education also stemmed from the fact that out of 420-plus employees, when I first joined the fire department, few had degrees. I only knew of one. I thought education would assist me with promotions. Little did I know what a quantum leap of promotion would later occur.

My pursuit of a college education began in the spring semester of 1970 at age twenty-three. I enrolled in my first two classes, extemporaneous speaking and college English. Those courses helped me effectively express myself in written and oral forms. Now, looking back on a forty-five-year association with the fire service, I find the most successful individuals communicated effectively.

The speech and English classes provided lifelong lessons and skills. A professor who made me think taught the speech class. His midterm exam seemed simple and straightforward. "To every rule, there's an exception, true or false?" I never forgot his lessons on reasoning and a different way of looking at things.

The English class began a long-term process that ended with a teaching certificate. I thought that substitute teaching might provide yet another part-time job opportunity. I'm sure it's apparent by now that the grammar portion didn't interest me. However, the literature did, particularly British and American writers. I enjoyed interpreting poetry. That naturally led to a desire for research that uncovered the truth behind the beauty of a well-written poem—which taught me how to deeply ponder the words. Although I liked the sounds and images poets provided, what were they telling me? This question made me look beyond the obvious. I employ those same techniques today when my favorite lyrical poets release a new song.

The problem with our educational system begins with the fact that we have forgotten the basic purpose of education. The purpose isn't to teach *what* to think, rather *how* to think! Just because students can memorize what educators want them to remember doesn't mean students have learned how to think. There will be more on this, but I will not vary from that basic premise. Educating students on how to think should be a strategy. A good tactic supporting that strategy would pay preschool and kindergarten teachers more than other teachers instead of treating them like entry-level babysitters. If a how-to-think education strategy isn't taught effectively early on, thinking skills might never fully occur for some. Those who have developed good how-to-think skills will always be in greater demand in any organization. An application of those skills to managing emergencies would be welcome in any organization that needs problems solved.

Wichita State had a lecture series, but I only attended a few because of my schedule. One guest lecturer and author ended up doing well. I went to his lecture because of a book he wrote, *The Sirens of Titan*. My interest in his book derived from one line: "I can think of no more stirring symbol of man's humanity to man than a fire engine." The author, Kurt Vonnegut Jr., had a way with humor that made me think.

Throughout the next couple of years, 1970–72, I pursued my education, union activities, firefighting, and saving lives and property. In 1972, the union helped create a degree program in fire science at Wichita State University. Along with that degree program, firefighters could branch out into other areas such as management, accounting, and education. All those skill sets are valuable in any organization.

Ranking officers of the department had tried unsuccessfully to secure a degree program, so the deputy chief of operations let me try.

Almost all my efforts included communication with the deputy chief of operations. My goal began with a simple request to the president of the university. He summarily passed me off to the vice president for academic affairs, who gave me the preliminary runaround by suggesting we contact a vocational-technical school. I mentioned the union membership had grown tired of hearing about the vocational-technical concept because we provided our own entry-level training. We got nowhere fast.

Shortly after that, I relayed this story to a city commissioner, who made me aware of a one-half mill tax levy on property. The city of Wichita gave that money to the university each year. Two days later I sat in the VP's dark-wood-paneled office that adjoined the president's office. He had a somber countenance that matched his five o'clock shadow. He spoke in soft and gentle sentences that gave the appearance of concern. He slowly got to his point by asking, "Have you given any thought to the vocational-technical school idea?"

This time I began by making a passionate plea. "You know, our fathers came home from the war and wanted an education, sometimes funded through the G.I. Bill. Those veterans also wanted the same thing for their children, and a direct relationship existed between government and education. We don't want any funding consideration, only educational opportunities. As an urban fire department, we need an urban university education."

Before the VP dozed off, I calmly stated, "Some of our members want to start picketing the university, appear before the city commission, and ask for a repeal of the one-half mill levy tax gift to the university." I offered a question: "If the university isn't interested in supporting the city fire department, why should the city support the university?"

His eyes became a little more focused. He had endured picketing by the anti-war folk, but that hadn't involved a potential loss of revenue. "Let me visit with the engineering department and get back with you." I'm sure, afterward, he reflected on the more passionate part of my request. On December 1, 1972, the VP sent a letter to the fire department's deputy chief of operations: "At the request of Mr. Jim Sparr of your department…the dean of the College of Engineering has developed some courses, additional courses are possible, and members from the department can review the content…."

The deputy chief handed my copy to me and smiled. "How did you do that?"

"You don't want to know." As a gentle and patient man, he would not have approved of my stern tactics.

We had one more hoop to jump through. Awarding associate's and bachelor's degrees required consent of the total faculty. The packed auditorium included those professors against the proposal, who spoke about the value and sanctity of an intellectual education versus the kind where knowledge had practical applications. Those professors ignored the mantra across college campuses calling for educators to "make it relevant!"

After the what-to-think professors finished, a rotund math professor stood up. His white dress shirt strained the buttons over his belly, and both ends of his tie stopped well short of his trousers. Fashion missteps notwithstanding, communication skills prevailed. His opening remark was, "What jewel fell out of your crowns and tumbled down from the ivory tower?" The speech became more personal and practical from that point on. He pointed to the organizational goal of attracting more students and suggested that some of the new students might even branch out into more cerebral disciplines. After a round of applause, a voice vote affirmed our proposal.

Dr. John Leslie taught most of the fire science classes. He was a tall fellow who wore thick-lensed glasses with black frames. He looked like a stereotypical engineer only without a pen and pencil pocket protector. He had a down-to-earth speaking style and occasionally made some off-color comments. No professor could've been better suited for what he was about to experience. Many firefighters from all ranks participated because they saw a future where education would count for promotions. Professor Leslie visited fire stations and became familiar with what we did.

He also reviewed our study material. He challenged some of our long-held notions of hydraulics. One, in particular, noted a convoluted relationship between pounds of pressure and gallons of water known as pounds/gallons.

He stated, "No such thing exists." One of the department's finest training officers took umbrage at his statement but couldn't substantiate his case with facts. Those kinds of exchanges proved valuable to individuals and the department.

On another topic, our red book explained heat transfer. Conduction, convection, and radiation defined the three methods of heat transfer. Heat conducted through metal doorknobs, so we avoided taking hold of one when a fire burned in a room. The same principle applied when grabbing the handle of a hot pan. We had concentrated on heat flowing to us.

Dr. Leslie asked, "How many of you have ever stepped from the carpet onto a tile floor with your bare feet and felt the tile's coldness?" Most of the class, including me, raised our hands.

"How much colder is the tile compared to the carpet?"

Before we made fools of ourselves, he stated, "The temperature's the same for the tile and carpet, but the carpet acts as a better insulator, and therefore heat leaves our feet more quickly on tile than carpet." His lesson on heat flowing away from us reinforced the law of heat transfer. Heat always flows from a warm to a cold source. That's a key element in how to think about fire travel.

That how-to-think professor made us think. He also provided a worthwhile piece of organizational advice that I've never forgotten: "Don't kick the butt today you may have to kiss tomorrow." Other firefighters later reflected on that statement.

I graduated cum laude on December 20, 1974, with a BA in education including a major in secondary education in English and a double minor in engineering and education. Earning my teaching certificate required student teaching, some at Wichita South High School and some at North High School.

I remember a general assembly that took place during my student teaching time at South High School. A guest lecturer named Maya Angelou had written *I Know Why the Caged Bird Sings*. I read her book because it was part of an English class assignment. Her description of foods like cornmeal and buttermilk, watermelon, and homemade ice cream took me back to my younger days in Joplin, Missouri. She brought back the taste and smell of each item with her descriptions of sensory images.

Ms. Angelou also painted a picture of the human condition I had not seen. She used terms that described white folk that I had only heard used to describe black folk. She had no fear of having a serious discussion on race relations. Her story was persuasive because she lived through all of it, but her way of communicating injustices allowed the reader to feel them as well.

Her lecture focused on the maturation of a young African American male. Ms. Angelou said, "An immature male slouches and swaggers this way. A more mature man carries himself this way." She demonstrated her point by walking and posturing through the growth process. She educated both prejudiced posture-critics and African

American immature males. She made people think, and her melodic deep-toned voice resonated with precise wording and held people captive to her message.

Years later I thoroughly enjoyed seeing her give a reading at the inauguration of President Clinton. Hearing how much she had accomplished in her life thus far, given her beginnings, and seeing the impact she had on other people's lives amazed me. I heard of her passing while working on a draft of this book in 2014. Her message of hope inspired many, including me. Ms. Angelou was one of two African Americans who changed my behavior and thinking about racial issues.

Sam Cooke also had an influence on me, derived from one song in particular: "A Change Is Gonna Come." The seeds of rock and roll planted in the late 1950s flourished in the 1960s and 1970s. Young people learned about racism, and the virtues of peace, love, and understanding through Motown artists. Young people learned how to think about racism from musical artists and authors like Maya Angelou—not politicians. White singers covered black artists' work and thereby drew more attention to the original works and artists. But Sam Cooke attracted a following on his own and broke down some racial barriers with that one song. I learned to concentrate on an individual's substance rather than their appearance.

The remainder of my student teaching occurred at North High School. That's where I had graduated in 1964 with a D+ average for what to think. I saw my grade point average as a C– for learning how to think. The senior student body had elected me prom king, but my grade average fell below the required minimum, so I forfeited that distinction. Of course it was my own fault, but at the time I viewed that experience as government (school board) thwarting the will of the people (senior student body).

I reflected on my old high school days, where our mascot was a culturally dressed Native American and the students were proud Redskins. My distinguishing feat in the Indian Ways competition involved maneuvering a canoe without a paddle. To accomplish that skill, tribesmen usually stood with bare feet on the gunnels (edges) at one end of a canoe and bounced up and down, moving the canoe forward. Until attending North, I always played a cowboy when playing cowboys and Indians. Now I thought about overcoming adversity and the advantages of starting from a position of perceived weakness. Instead of taking offense, I enjoyed people underestimating me. *As you take the low road, please wait in the Little Bighorn valley below. I'll take the high road down and join you shortly.*

I graduated with pride as a North High Redskin. Blackbear Bosin was our tribal chief. The finest Native American artist that ever lived, Blackbear Bosin created a tile art piece that hung in the main hallway by the administrative offices. Over fifty years have passed, but I remember one thing about that art piece. Blackbear Bosin purposely left a small imperfection, which I never found. As a man of faith, he claimed that humanity was imperfect and that only a higher being was capable of perfection. I don't remember much about my academic failures or successes at that institution, but I remember that statement.

I also remember a piece of Indian folklore on how there will never be a tornado at the confluence of two rivers. Major devastation from tornados occurred in communities around Wichita, but miles from that confluence. That specific site seemed a wise choice for the Mid-America All-Indian Center.

Returning to the role of student teacher, I taught a module on poetry and chose a technique relating to all young students. Some students didn't like poetry, but all students liked music. For a practical application, I chose two songs. One was the Paul Simon song "Mother and Child Reunion," the other Led Zeppelin's "Stairway to Heaven." I provided a copy of the words and played the 45 rpm vinyl on a record player. My supervising teacher must've liked my performance because she provided a report that described my efforts as "extraordinary," a word never used to describe my job performance before or since. I later used my teaching techniques as an adjunct instructor and incorporated them into my management style. I always tried gaining people's attention first, then encouraged broader thinking.

One year after my undergraduate efforts, work began on my graduate degree. I completed my undergraduate degree in five years and my master's in seven and a half years. Most students completed their graduate work in two years, but they didn't hold down a full-time job, spend time with children on weekends, do union work, and teach fire science classes at Wichita State and Hutchinson Community College. Finally, I got to use my teaching certificate. I became an adjunct instructor, which meant and paid little, but gave me valuable knowledge and an impressive résumé.

I taught a wide variety of courses: Industrial Fire Safety, Construction Methods and Materials (under fire conditions), Introduction to Fire Protection and Suppression, Fundamentals of

Fire Prevention, Fire Protection Systems, Firefighting Tactics and Strategy, Fire Service Administration I, and Special Topics—Fire Administration. Teaching a course required more study than taking a course. Those courses kept me on the leading edge of each discipline and served me well later in my career.

In 1981 I finally received a master's of urban affairs (MUA) degree from the Urban Affairs Department. A few years after I finished, the title changed to master of public administration (MPA). Somebody made an inquiry about the possibility of the MUA title change to MPA for those who graduated with an MUA, even if it required additional work. Several people joined in the simple and straightforward request.

Although some MUA graduates may have had an urban affair or two, none considered themselves masters. The MPA degree seemed more marketable for job applications than an MUA degree. A compromise included a statement on our transcript that the title change took place.

I know why some people denied the original MPA title and will share that secret now. The Board of Regents, located in Topeka, met near Kansas University. KU had a group of city manager graduates called "kucimags," which stood for KU city managers. That clandestine organization selfishly held on to the MPA degree and humiliated other state universities, like Wichita State, by forcing the MUA degree on them. At least that's the story I told when around my kucimag, Gene Denton.

Sounding the acronym "MUA" reminded me of one of those dairy cows I milked, only with a foreign accent. As one can see, I still haven't gotten over the scars of that degreed title. That's why to this day I ask KU graduates if they are still handicapped in their thinking ability because of an education that taught them what to think, rather than how. I also ask what that ugly crow mascot is all about.

Finally, nobody could tell me what to display on the ring I paid for, so mine has "MPA" engraved on it. So there.

13

I Love a Parade

Fire Station 10, a one-story red brick building, had a basement under the living quarters. The inside walls, as in all stations, had a light color of institutional green paint. There was a hose storage area in the basement and an area with a Ping-Pong table, another forum for competition between firefighters. I had average success at Ping-Pong, but the routine trouncing provided by co-workers Jim and Doug helped develop my hand-eye coordination. Jim was a little pudgy around the middle, but quick on his feet. He had a space in his upper teeth, third from the middle, that occasionally held his cigarette. He did it because it drove Doug crazy. I always knew when the ritual began because Jim looked at me and moved his head backward one time as if to say, "*Watch this.*" He placed the cigarette's filter in the space between his teeth just before gaining Doug's attention.

"Why do you do that?"

"Do what?"

"You know what I'm talking about."

"No, I was just minding my own business," Jim said, as he grinned widely with the cigarette still lodged in its resting place. He then looked at me. "Do you know what he's talking about?"

"I don't have a clue," I said, and joined Jim's laughter when Doug left the room, shaking his head.

Doug was tall, had a lean frame and a premature receding hairline, and loved competing. He took revenge on the basement Ping-Pong table.

Up a flight of concrete stairs from the basement, the ground level of the station had a captain's office/television room, bunkroom, locker room, kitchen, and restroom. Those restroom sinks were where my "Ajax theory of management" from a subordinate point of view took shape. Two ramps sloped downward from the living quarters to the single bay that housed a pumper. Those ramps with rubber matting proved safer than steps.

We had a telephone in the kitchen, and two in the captain's office/ television room. The departmental phone line sat on the captain's office desk, and the television room had a personal line for firefighters. A phone extension for the firefighters sat on the kitchen countertop. If we all gathered in the kitchen and the captain's phone rang, we ran from the kitchen to the office and answered it. To avoid that unsafe practice, for years we tried having a departmental extension line installed in the kitchen. One can guess what my first directive was when promoted to a position of authority. Later, I also had that facility expanded for housing a quick response vehicle, primarily for medical calls in an underserved community.

Station 10 occasionally was a punishment assignment. Some newly promoted captains, however, rotated through there for experience before being transferred to a two-company facility. As a result, captains changed frequently. Just when we had one trained, he moved on. One such captain, nicknamed the "Ajax captain," seemed cool. Beside his Greek god build, sandy hair, blue eyes, and impeccable appearance, he nitpicked assignments. Once he took hold of something, he wouldn't let go, even after making his point.

One time he noticed some paint specks on my hands from a painting job the day before. He abruptly told me, "Make yourself presentable." I tried, but the paint thinner wouldn't remove specks from around my cuticles and under my fingernails. The third attempt, including a small container of gasoline and a wire brush, worked. While I was diligently complying with a direct order, our district chief drove up. He exited his vehicle, asked what I was doing, smiled at my answer, and went inside. A moment later the captain came outside and, without looking at my fingers, said, "That's good enough."

Captain Ajax just thought I had a hard head. But Doug would argue with a signpost and take the wrong way home. On Fridays, we mowed the lawn. One Friday the captain told Doug, "Mow the lawn."

"I will," Doug said.

Sometime later the captain told him again, and Doug said he would. That behavior on the part of a firefighter had two labels: "bulling" or "bowing one's neck." I understood the bull metaphor, but never fully understood the neck bowing. I mentioned the captain's lawn-mowing goal might be achieved more quickly if he asked our co-worker what he thought would be a good time for lawn mowing. Jim couldn't wait for that approach and chimed in. "Yeah, why don't you try that, Captain?"

The captain chose another approach. He told Doug, "I should send you home without pay for insubordination, but you probably wouldn't go. I am, however, going to consider it." A few moments later we heard the lawn mower.

Another incident with Captain Ajax occurred one time when we received a new flashlight that needed painting with the district and company colors. The colors identified equipment when several trucks at an emergency scene had scattered equipment.

As the driver for that shift, he told me, "Take a piece of sandpaper and rough up the slick surface so the paint will adhere." I completed sanding and painting in the precise place on the flashlight as instructed. Captain Ajax checked my work and called me out to the vehicle bay for a dissertation on properly preparing a surface for paint. I kept reaching for the flashlight to comply with the captain's wishes and end the dissertation, of which I had grown a little tired. Every time I reached for the flashlight, he pulled it away and continued.

Finally, Captain Ajax handed over the flashlight. "Sand the paint off and redo it." Then I sanded the new flashlight so deep it had what looked like a tiny mouse bite out of the front end. About an hour later I heard my name called from the lecture hall, also known as the vehicle bay.

Only so many ways existed of responding to "Why did you do that?" After exhausting all my known responses, most of which rephrased, "Because you told me to," I felt like the time had arrived for moving on with our lives and started walking away.

Much to my surprise, Captain Ajax followed me with his verbal inquisition. We circled the fire truck twice, and then I led the miniparade up the ramp and past the kitchen door. Inside the kitchen my two co-workers, nice guy Jim and hardhead Doug, both grinned from ear to ear. We proceeded into the bunkroom, through the television room, down the other ramp, and back out onto the bay floor. About the time we began our circle around the truck again, the captain stopped, placed the flashlight in the truck, and told me, "Never do that again." Later, I asked which one of my co-workers left Ajax residue on the sink that morning but received no answer.

Both Jim and Doug were tough interior-attack firefighters and all three of us took pride in our busy station assignment. We responded to many varied situations. Inside one house fire it felt and sounded like large raindrops hitting the tops of our helmets. After the smoke cleared, we could see the raindrops were dying cockroaches falling from the ceiling.

The hottest interior firefight occurred in the 1500 block of Washington Street. Sometime after midnight two electronic tones sounded in the bunkroom and all station lights came on. Jim, Doug, Captain Ajax, and I threw the covers back and put on bunker gear next to our beds. Like four slow-motion zombies we made our way through the bunkroom door and down the rubber-treaded ramp, and then donned our remaining protective gear. Doug and I stepped up on the tailboard and clicked our safety belts shut. Captain Ajax pushed the button that opened the overhead front door.

The 911 dispatcher always delayed announcing the type of alarm and address for a few seconds. This let firefighters concentrate on safely getting ready for responding. By then groggy minds had cleared enough for concentrating on a message. "Still alarm for engine 10. Check for unknown cause of smoke in the 1500 block of North Washington Street." The dispatcher then repeated the information. Jim climbed into the driver's seat, turned on the emergency lights, and started the pumper's engine. Captain Ajax waited while Jim drove the pumper onto the front concrete slab, activated the door closer, climbed into the fire truck, and fastened his seat belt. We turned south on Grove Street and increased our speed. No cars were on the street, so Captain Ajax didn't activate the wind siren until we turned onto Thirteenth Street.

As we picked up speed, the rushing wind and siren noise made hearing difficult. Doug shouted, "It's probably someone burning trash." I nodded in agreement. That seemed like a safe guess because many area residents couldn't afford trash collection, so they burned trash and garbage in fifty-five-gallon drums.

When we got to Washington Street and turned north we saw the haze of smoke beneath streetlights that looked like ground fog on a damp fall evening. In general, white smoke indicated a field fire; black smoke indicated a petroleum-based fire, like burning roofing materials. The gray color of smoke ahead indicated burning wood and other building materials. Smoke also had distinct smells. Doug and I caught the scent about the same time. We looked like two wine connoisseurs in a tasting facility as we took a couple of sniffs. "That's not a trash fire," I said. Doug agreed.

Captain Ajax let off the siren, and Jim slowed to a crawl as we searched both sides of the street for the fire's origin. Then on the right side we saw a concrete-block building with a loading dock. Smoke poured out from the eaves, which meant the fire might or might not have spread to the attic.

Jim pulled into the parking lot a good distance from the building in case the fire got out of control. A ladder company could then position close to the building and pour gallons of water on a roofless lost cause. The old saying went like this: "When the ladder goes up, the building is coming down."

Captain Ajax pressed the radio mic button: "Engine 10, this is a code three fire. Make this a regular alarm."

The dispatcher's "Ten-four, Engine 10" acknowledgment meant two more pumpers, a ladder truck, and a district chief would soon respond. Captain Ajax and I started pulling hose for an attack, while Jim and Doug connected hose to a nearby fire hydrant for a sustained water supply. Both tasks finished about the same time as Doug turned the hydrant on that expanded flat hose to the fire truck's pump intake. Captain Ajax shouted, "Put three air-pack cases on the loading dock!" Jim and Doug opened a truck compartment door, grabbed the air-pack cases, and laid them on the loading dock.

Doug joined Captain Ajax and me on the loading dock as we laid out enough S-shaped hose line for the interior attack. I turned the exterior door's handle so it opened. I thought, *Remember this for the investigator because it could be the work of an arsonist*. There was an immediate rush of air into the building through the one-inch door opening because the fire used up needed oxygen and desperately wanted more. The pressure from the inward rush of air pulled the door shut. That's when we heard a couple of loud pops. Shortly thereafter a couple more: "POW! POW!" I immediately thought, *Spalling*. Spalling occurs when concrete heats to a temperature that turns moisture into steam so that small chunks explode from the concrete's surface.

Then it happened again, only this time: "POW! BUZZ, POW! SIZZLE." In unison we all said, "Electricity." Captain Ajax walked to the building's corner and saw the incoming electrical line as it sizzled, burned, and fell away from the building. "Okay, we're good to go." We donned our air tanks, connected the mask hoses to the tanks, simultaneously turned the tank valves on, and secured our face masks. We then secured our helmets.

Doug gave the thumbs-up to Jim, who charged the fire hose line with water. I opened the nozzle as Captain Ajax propped the door open. A whooshing sound of air poured into the building. A *varoom* sound made brilliant red, yellow, and orange colors come alive. We faced our full-blown enemy.

I got down on one knee and tightly gripped the nozzle. Doug was on the other side of the hose line and also got down on one knee. We fanned the water weapon from side to side and made our forward charge. Captain Ajax was behind us, pulling hose. The initial blast of water created total darkness, and we felt the heat roll above our heads and out the open door. The easy part was over. We began the final hard charge that would drive the enemy to the back of the building and extinguish the last large flames. It seemed like a long time passed as I concentrated on slow breathing. We took a lot of heat. I felt the sting from minor burns on my exposed ears.

That's when I noticed my entire body felt soaked to the bone. It couldn't be from water because I was behind the nozzle and fully dressed. Then some of the oozing moisture rolled over my mouth and I tasted the salt. The same protective clothing that kept heat out also kept heat in. My sweat-drenched body felt dizzy and nauseated. I knew instantly what was happening.

The first time I experienced heat exhaustion occurred on a hot summer day while baling hay. The farmer drove the tractor and baler while I stood on the trailer, picked up the bales as they came out of the baler, and stacked them four rows high on the trailer. Sweat poured from my body, my mouth was dry, and I felt nauseated. We had one small row left and I tried to stick it out, but the farmer saw what was happening. He stopped the tractor and came back to the trailer with a jug of water. He lifted the jug over me, opened the spigot, and poured water over my head. "That should cool you off a little bit. Now, drink this," as he handed me a tin cup of water. As I rested in a tree's shade, the farmer stacked the remaining bales. We drove back to the farmyard and my workday was over.

I knew what was needed, but Doug and Captain Ajax also needed me. My male ego prevented my showing any hint of weakness or quitting. I closed the nozzle as a couple of muffled sentences made it past my air mask. "I don't want to hog all the fun. You take the nozzle."

"Okay." Doug felt his way to the front as I positioned myself between him and Captain Ajax. Doug opened the nozzle, and we made the final push. Although my energy requirement had lessened, cooling off, hydrating, and relaxing became a must to avoid puking and passing out. I heard the sirens of the other fire trucks arriving.

Captain Ajax shouted muffled sentences through his air mask. "I think we got most of it. Let's take a breather and let the other crews finish up." After Doug shut the nozzle off, both he and Captain Ajax began walking bent over, feeling the hose on their way to the door. I put the hose between my knees and began crawling out, shallow breathing, and stopping along the way. I finally saw faded light coming through the door and heard Captain Ajax cautioning everyone about the downed power line behind the building. The district chief radioed the dispatcher and requested a response from the electric company. That would have normally been handled before we made our attack if we had responded together, as part of many required simultaneous operational considerations.

I heard someone yelling, "Have the truck company make an opening in the back of the building for cross-ventilation." I thought, *That would've been nice before we made our attack.*

Just then Doug's silhouette appeared in the doorway. "Jim."

"I'm right here."

Doug came over and knelt down beside me. "What's the matter?"

I pulled my air mask off and told him what was happening. "Don't say anything. Just help me outside and get me some water." Doug held my air tank. That way it looked like he was helping take off my air tank, which he did when we reached the loading dock. I took off my fire coat, and Doug sprayed water over my head from a backup hose line on the dock. That immediately cooled me down. Then Doug semiclosed the nozzle, and I drank water like a camel at a newly found oasis. I sat down and leaned against the loading dock wall.

Doug sat down next to me. "Wow! That's the hottest one I've ever fought."

"Me too."

I closed my eyes and began the relaxing technique of a concentrated slower heart rate while recalling what we just did. The pride in extreme task accomplishment and daily humor at Station 10 made these the best days of my professional life.

Another captain stationed there, Tom Massey, became someone I admired. Tom had a stout frame and weighed over two hundred pounds. He enjoyed eating, Italian food in particular. As a result of excessive food intake, he sported a nice round belly. Tom had always scored high on promotional examinations. I decided to take the promotional exam for lieutenant, and Captain Massey said he would gladly help me. He said he would "push me," meaning he would hound his boss on my behalf. He said he would also give me a good rating if I earned it.

Most of all I liked Tom's sense of humor. The morning he arrived at Station 10 we stood in the kitchen, visiting with an off-going crew as we awaited their departure. The phone behind us rang, so Tom answered it. "Fire Station 10, this is Massey."

One of our citizens called the wrong number but didn't miss an opportunity at humor. The citizen said in a loud voice, "Massey, what is a Massey?" The citizen then asked, "Massey, do you know what you are?"

"No," Tom politely answered, as he held the phone away from his ear.

"Massey, you are a dumbass," he said and hung the phone up.

We heard a smoker's wheezing exhale build to full-throated laughter. Tears came to his eyes when Tom laughed hard. His teary eyes became my gauge as to how much brief joy I gave him. It turned out that Tom enjoyed dark or even sick humor, as did I. Many a night I woke him up at home with jokes someone told me. He called those jokes "rotters," meaning rotten. If one sounded particularly sick, he said, "Oh, that's a real rotter," then began laughing loudly.

Tom also had an intense emotional response when something didn't go as he thought it should. I shared his predilection for the extremes of humor and anger and knew when he was angry. It started with Tom taking hold of the right side of his glasses with his thumb and forefinger behind the eyepiece. He removed the eyeglasses in slow motion and said, "I'm going to tell you something." I witnessed that mannerism twice and recognized that someone better pay attention.

I first noticed Tom's mannerism on an alarm response at Wichita State University. A student struck an electrical pole with her car, and power lines lay on the ground. When we arrived on scene, an important person representing the university, the director of the physical plant, greeted us. We knew of his importance because he told us so. He determined the situation was under control and we could leave.

Captain Massey informed the Important Person, "You need to step back to a safe area until we confirm the scene safety." Important Person informed Captain Massey that we all stood on state property, and as such he had jurisdiction, backed up by state law. That's when I noticed the slow-motion removal of glasses. Jim moved to the front of the fire truck, while Doug and I got quickly to curbside.

The information that followed went like this: "I'm going to tell you something. We are standing on a city street, and if you don't step back, I'm going to have you arrested for interference, and you can sort the jurisdictional issue out from a jail cell."

Important Person started mumbling something about campus police versus city police.

Captain Massey moved a little closer to Important Person. "Now!"

The exhibition of command presence worked. We finished our task and returned to the station. Captain Massey knew who would get blamed if we left early and something went wrong. I remembered that later in my career when challenged by a bullying politician. Also, I had an encounter with Important Person over an examination of construction plans that Tom Massey would have loved.

The other time I witnessed Captain Massey's mannerism, strangely enough, happened with our district chief. My cumulative score from the lieutenant's examination, performance rating, and interview panel placed my name high on the promotional list. True to his word, Captain Massey followed our district chief outside and asked him whom he was pushing. The district chief went over his choices, and then it happened. The glasses slowly came off, and here's what the district chief heard after the preliminary setup: "You don't have another choice. Let me tell you why." Tom ticked off a litany of my accomplishments compared to the other candidates.

As it turned out, my promotion recommendation came straight from the fire chief. A hint came while we sat in a pension board meeting, considering a retirement application for a lieutenant. Because I filled an elected board position and because he was fire chief, we both voted on all retirement applications. The chief leaned over and asked if I saw a potential conflict of interest in voting on that application because, after a few promotions, my name was now on top of the promotional list. My response was "You tell me," because the fire chief could recommend a candidate from any position on the list.

He smiled, and we concluded our pension board business. Not long after, our district chief showed up at Station 10 and announced my promotion to lieutenant. He said he knew it would happen, just not this soon, and that no officer to date had received a promotion out of Station 10. Even my co-worker Jim transferred to a headquarters station before his lieutenant promotion.

My new station assignment sent me back to 500 South Topeka, Fire Station No. 2.

I never forgot my time at Station 10. As previously mentioned, the community had been embroiled in racial conflicts a few years earlier. Poverty and its companion, crime, were other social issues that plagued many neighbors. Hardworking people like Linda, who owned a liquor store across the street from Fire Station 10, did their best to make a decent living. We watched through the wall of kitchen windows as she closed in the evenings. Firefighters noticed anyone entering the store with malicious intentions, and more importantly, they could see us watching.

Paying attention to residents around me and university reading helped bring about an appreciation for other peoples' challenges and points of view. English professors like Dr. John Poe, whom I nicknamed Edgar, gave me thought-provoking reading assignments. Open and frank discussions on a variety of social issues dominated our lunch conversations outside of the classroom. Between my service at Station 10 and my university studies, I learned life's best personal and professional lessons.

One of my fondest job memories at Station 10 involved driving the fire truck. The accompanying picture shows a pumping operation at the Sutherland lumberyard fire. The photo indicates a normal pumping operation with studious monitoring of pressure gauges. The district chief came up and asked if I knew the next hydrant location because the one I pumped from was on the list as out of service. "Have you had any pressure problems?"

I felt my stomach churn a little bit as I timidly pointed to a hydrant one block away. "No, Chief, I haven't noticed any problems, but I'll communicate any problems immediately." After firefighters extinguished the all-night fire, we returned to our station early the next morning. Captain Massey first checked the chalkboard in the kitchen. The department expected us to keep track of nonworking hydrants until they were repaired, but one of the other shifts hadn't placed the hydrant status on the chalkboard. Some firefighters never missed an opportunity to blame another shift. Thank goodness they didn't record the nonfunctioning hydrant and that the water department had repaired the hydrant that day, or I would have left the station with a little of my posterior missing.

Sutherland Lumber Fire

14

MUSICAL NOTES

My first day as a lieutenant at Station 2 made me reflect on my first week there as a rookie. The interaction between personnel and different ranks seemed similar. I knew most of the personnel at Station 2, except for a couple of younger guys and a rookie. One lieutenant, in particular, worked with me at that facility before and still knew the art of razor-edge knife sharpening. Lieutenant Bo's forearm and shoulder muscles appeared as solid as his reputation for being an aggressive interior-attack firefighter. I knew about that reputation because I had fought fire with him before. On one of his days off, he received a commendation for his heroic efforts in extinguishing a fire that occurred in a small community away from Wichita.

Lieutenant Bo understood fire behavior and always investigated new firefighting techniques. That rare combination separated him from other aggressive interior-attack firefighters because most of them suffered from the "candle-moth syndrome." That's to say, when they saw a flame, they went for it. Lieutenant Bo considered factors such as fire travel and the extra damage or danger to others if ventilation didn't occur before extinguishment. He understood that if two companies attacked a fire from different directions, they could push flames onto each other.

Lieutenant Bo knew the proper use of an elevating ladder truck, and all the damage and danger caused when it was used improperly. He could quickly calculate how many gallons per minute of water flowed into a building. That, combined with the weight of one gallon of water, told him the total weight that flowed into a structure. He used those quick calculations for cautioning an impending floor collapse. Most of all, he understood that different types of construction had different burn times before the structure failed and collapsed. Those burn times told him when exposed buildings needed covering or when to keep firefighters safely back and give up on the building fire, letting it burn out.

His personal experience and textbook knowledge made him the perfect candidate for a training officer. The same chief who recommended my promotion later recommended Bo's promotion to that position. He eventually became my point man for innovation and change concerning firefighting tactics and strategy.

Now that Lieutenant Bo has been properly established as an icon who could hold Prometheus at bay, let me say that his day-to-day behavior around the fire station differed. He loved practical jokes and water fights in particular. He always carried a glass of water around, and I knew that he didn't use it for hydrating himself.

Water wars usually started with a few tiny drops of water that accidentally fell from a glass that overhung from a second-story window. That unfortunate escape of water always landed on some poor fellow standing below.

It takes a certain kind of person to run into a burning building in fight mode when most regular people would run away in full flight. But it became a problem when that aggressive mentality carried over into daily activities. It's only natural that a return volley contained six tiny droplets, whereas the initial incident had only three.

One Saturday morning, ten years earlier, I witnessed the water wars escalating to a new height. Firefighter Mike, the same person who told me about the job while sitting by the pool, and Lieutenant Bo enjoyed pranks. One of them fired the initial salvo.

As with any conflict, some collateral damage occurred. A young muscle-bound horse named Butch joined the wet-and-wild adventure. Butch grabbed Mike from behind, and with a mighty exhibition of force, he slowly squeezed the air from Mike's lungs. Butch gave clear instructions. He told someone, "Take a bucket, fill it from the mop sink, and throw the bucket of water on Mike."

That's where my memory fades because I don't remember who slowly filled the bucket while the poor prisoner awaited his fate. Someone tossed the bucket of water. Firefighter Mike, no shrinking violet, remained unusually calm. As water left the bucket, Mike's strategy became clear. He jerked his head to the right side so water would drench the young stallion behind him. Butch reacted by yanking Mike back in place. That's when the bucket came in contact with the left side of Mike's face, at the eyebrow. When someone takes a blow there, it bleeds.

At that moment we caught a four-tone alert, which meant a structure fire in progress. The four-tone alert meant our station would empty all vehicles and personnel. That day I rode the back tailboard of Engine 2 along with Mike.

After we safely boarded, Captain Seaman climbed into the pumper and we headed west. As we proceeded on our emergency run, we crossed McLean Boulevard and the railroad tracks. When trucks crossed those tracks at a higher speed, it created a springboard effect, which propelled tailboard riders into the air, depending on the flexing of knees. The bounce made Captain Seaman turn around and check on the tailboard riders. That's when he noticed blood and water running down the side of Mike's face. He did a double take and kept his eyes on Mike.

After extinguishing a garage fire under an apartment and cleaning up debris, we returned to quarters. Captain Seaman lined everyone up for a lecture on water fights that mistakenly included these words: "It's okay if you throw cold water on a guy if he's in the shower." That was the only part of the lecture we remembered. Someone suggested that since I knew the captain for years, I should be the sacrificial lamb who threw cold water on the captain during his evening shower.

Any such endeavor required careful planning, such as where to get a large volume of cold water. We cooked ham and beans in a large pot every Saturday on duty. I filled the large pot with water and ice cubes and placed it in the refrigerator. That night, when the soaped-up captain couldn't see, I heaved the pot of cold water on him. The loud gasping for air was heard throughout the upper floor as firefighters disappeared to other parts of the station. When he stopped gasping and cleared his eyes, I reminded him of his earlier statement.

Later that evening Captain Seaman found me and quietly said, "You should be more careful about being influenced by others." He too knew about "Bo the instigator," another of his known tags.

"I will, Captain. Thank you."

Ten years later, the iconic Lieutenant Bo hadn't lost a step. Water accidents continued, but not to the same degree as before. We had a new captain, and he didn't share the same tolerance for water accidents. He busted us one time and told us to knock it off.

The second time Bo, the offending party, was caught red-handed. I thought, *You finally got caught.*

However, with a straight face he told the captain about a "trip spill." Bo calmly explained that he had tripped, and the water had spilled from his glass.

"That didn't look like a trip spill to me."

"Well, it was." Trip spills became a common occurrence.

As mentioned earlier, we cooked ham and beans along with cornbread every Saturday. I still recall having cornbread and ham and beans with my grandmother. She also put cornbread in a glass of buttermilk as Maya Angelou did with her cornmeal. I found that with a lot of salt I tolerated that concoction, but never got fully into it. Ham, cornbread, and beans remain one of my favorite food choices.

The only problem with firehouse beans and cornbread became noticeable later that evening. As with everything else, competition surfaced. Compared to the juvenile cowboys in *Blazing Saddles*, the more mature firefighters developed competition for:

- the longest note sounded,
- the most notes sounded, and
- the best change of pitch.

That last one required great care and absolute muscle control. The district chief at Station 10, who told me of my promotion to lieutenant, had legendary achievements for the longest note sounded. I approached the challenge, as usual, by focusing on the most difficult: change of pitch.

Other than my nonprofessional achievements, the challenge I enjoyed most was keeping training sessions fresh and memorable. I enjoyed training and emergency responses and knew the importance of using teaching techniques that stimulated the learning process. I achieved success when others remembered those training sessions or emergency responses years later.

One such training activity recalled by others involved familiarization with a new aerial ladder truck. Simply stated, the aerial had a long ladder with a metal basket on its end. When practicing, we drove the aerial ladder onto the concrete slab, set the outriggers for stability, and began the slow one-hundred-foot hydraulic climb upward. Setting the outrigger supports was critical because failure to do so was the cause for ladder trucks tipping over with disastrous results.

I always took a rookie with me, extending the ladder straight up to full height. I explained the importance of feathering the controls because the valving didn't work perfectly. While at the aerial's highest level, I said, "Now, here's what happens when you don't feather the controls," while slamming the control valve hard in one direction. Before the valve took hold, a few inches of free-fall swinging occurred. When the valve engaged, the entire ladder and basket rocked from side to side.

The widening of eyelids indicated concern as did the force of hands gripping handrails. If knuckles became white and eyes looked like silver dollars, concern transitioned to fear. I heard sounds and words that had only been heard on a late Saturday night, invoking the deities. When the rookies operated the controls for the first time, they demonstrated instant proficiency.

A memorable emergency response activity occurred when I went to Fire Station No. 1 and filled a temporary officer vacancy. The captain assigned me as an officer to rescue 1 company. We received an alarm for a man whose leg was trapped in a shut car door. It was my driver's first alarm. More often than not the accelerator foot involuntarily shook a little bit on a maiden voyage. That had happened on my first driving experience years before. The officer had me put the pedal to the metal and keep it there. That worked for me, but I tried something different with this young firefighter.

While underway with lights flashing and siren blaring, I reached over and put my hand on the young driver's leg. "I know we haven't known each other for long, but I feel close to you." After a quizzical glance in my direction, he returned his focus to the emergency response and his foot relaxed.

At the scene, we found a man who had tried exiting his parked vehicle facing a convenience store. The victim had opened his car door and placed his left foot outside. Before his foot touched the ground, another car pulled into an adjoining parking space and hit the open car door, slamming it shut with the driver's foot hanging out of the door's bottom. We used the "jaws of life" and popped the door open, and an immediate sigh of relief came over the man's face.

Upon returning to station quarters, my rescue vehicle driver kept retelling the story of my calming technique. That young firefighter eventually climbed to the top ladder rung with the Wichita Fire Department.

Lieutenant

15

PASS BLAME, ACCEPT CREDIT

At Station 2, most of us had many fun-filled days. The usual suspects included LJ, Pink, Loudy, Maxi, Lieutenant Bo and others guilty only by association, who will remain anonymous. All those men were fierce firefighting warriors who I would readily accompany into any dangerous situation.

Pink, one of those horse stereotypes, weighed more than 230 pounds, mostly muscle. One time, Pink picked up the front of a car and freed a trapped victim from underneath. I easily met the challenge of picking up a horse with Pink perched on my shoulders. Pink had only one constant complaint. Years before, in a money-saving move, the WFD installed toilet paper dispensers that dispensed five-inch-by-five-inch single sheets. The crusade for rolled toilet paper began with Loudy, and Pink was the first warrior who joined the cause. Loudy paraded around with a large stack of paper squares in one hand and a smaller amount of rolled paper in the other, proclaiming, "See, this practice actually costs more money!"

Pink joined the protest by displaying his own roll of paper and, except for the amount used during Loudy's campaign speeches, warned onlookers about the perils of stealing his coveted roll. The crusade proceeded without problems until Pink emerged from the restroom one evening before bedtime. As he exited the restroom in his tighty-whiteys and flip-flops, one end of the paper roll got caught in his shorts, which left a long paper trail to the roll in his hand.

Pink's saunter down the hall, as described by LJ, was the best-ever impression of a Chinese dragon. Later, as a suggestion for morale improvement, we replaced those containers with normal rolling dispensers. Loudy claimed that change marked our finest moment. Little creature comforts impressed employees.

Maxi, our cook, had a medium build and thinning dark-brown hair. Whether working in construction or in cooking, his hands always moved with the skill of a surgeon that matched his perfectionist approach to any task. I won't tell any stories on Maxi because he offered to be my corroborating witness on these stories, and I don't want a broken plate.

LJ, stoutly built, had coarse sandy hair and found irreverent humor in everything. He served verbal volleys that decapitated people, but they never realized it until they turned to walk away, without their head. LJ, like Lieutenant Bo, proudly carried the moniker of "instigator." LJ drove the district chief vehicle. LJ, as the district chief's boy, could say almost anything to him. Although the district chief appeared stern, his bite didn't match his bark. If he sensed weakness, trouble followed. If someone stood up to him nicely or humorously, they earned his respect. LJ somehow knew that instinctively.

Occasionally the district chief's bad mood manifested itself through a frown and eyes that searched for confrontation. That behavior dampened morale. When things looked a little bleak around the station, LJ said, "Come on, Chief, we need to go to Station 4." An officer at Station 4 seemed intimidated by the district chief. While en route there, LJ primed the pump on that officer and simultaneously extolled all our virtues by telling the district chief how lucky he was to have Station 2's crew. LJ sometimes told the district chief, "If you feel the need to yell at someone, yell at me." The district chief always smiled at LJ's comment because they both knew that would never happen.

Watching LJ's behavior, I decided someday if the need arose, I would replicate LJ's approach. My chance came the shift after a fire in a downtown apartment. We received an alarm for a building fire. That emptied the entire station. The district chief, Engine 2, Aerial 2, Truck 2, and Squad 2, the pumper that I was the officer on, responded. Upon arrival, we saw smoke coming from a second-story apartment on the rear of the building. A fire escape had a steel landing outside the second-story door and a sloping steel staircase to the ground.

After climbing the fire escape and gaining entry, we determined it was only a mattress fire. Pink brought a hand pump, which he could carry with one finger. Inside the five-gallon container of water, a bracket held a small glass jar of "wet water." To stifle cries of redundancy let me explain. The jar contained a slick substance similar to liquid soap. Those contents, when dumped into a hand pump, created a more penetrating liquid. We extinguished the mattress surface flames with the wetting agent. Heavy smoke from the deep smoldering mattress remained in the apartment, however, and ventilation didn't work.

I had Pink grab hold of one end of the mattress, while someone else held the other end. I wanted the smoldering mattress taken down the permanently attached steel fire escape steps to the alley, then opened up, and drowned with a booster line.

The red book correctly stated the three components required for flames: heat, fuel, and oxygen. Heat remained deep in the mattress, and the mattress provided fuel. The oxygen component was missing until halfway down the stairs when all components came together in a perfect mixture. As the mattress burst into flames, the two couriers quickened their pace. The firefighters both let go at the same time, and the cartwheeling mattress chased the lower quick-stepping firefighter to the bottom. Fortunately, the pyro display with sparks flying didn't catch him. That evening's entertainment was LJ's incessant retelling critique, each time with more embellishments.

I know beyond all doubt that the story reached the district chief's ears because the next duty-day morning, after roll call, he made a rare appearance with all ranks present. He had thick graying hair that he combed back and the overall appearance of a well-seasoned officer. After he paced back and forth in front of the troops a couple of times, he looked at the lined-up personnel. I thought, *He's going to compliment us on the alacrity with which we completed our task from the previous shift.* That didn't happen.

The soliloquy began with "That last shift had the worst operation I've ever seen."

After a few minutes, that old feeling of temper started creeping in. I sensed the blood flowing to my head. The district chief paused, and before he took another full breath, I asked, "May I see you in your office?"

"I guess so."

Everyone went their separate ways. I followed the district chief into his office.

I knew he and the deputy chief didn't get along. I began the conversation. "How would you like it if I went to the deputy chief and complained about something you did?"

"I wouldn't like it."

We then discussed his undercutting the authority of the captain, all the other officers, and me. We discussed the importance of chain of command. I told him that I ordered the mattress removed, so others shouldn't endure his shotgun verbal discipline. I told him I ordered the mattress removed because total extinguishment wasn't working and firefighters were taking a beating under the conditions. Only someone in the room could assess the situation, and I didn't just speak up during his speech because that would have undercut his authority. The conversation ended with my asking him to come directly to me, or better yet, go through the captain if he had any other similar issues. He smiled and said, "That sounds fair." From that moment on we got along fine.

From that exchange came a saying that went something like this: "Never accept blame when you can pass it along." The corollary follows: "Never give credit when you can take it." Of course, the message I sent meant just the opposite.

People of substance with character accept blame and give credit when it's due.

16

Customer Service

A character-building incident occurred on one of my off-duty days that would eventually use up all my accumulated sick leave. The weakened anterior cruciate ligament of my right knee, an issue that began with high school gymnastics injuries, finally took its toll. While playing racquetball, I reinjured my knee. But this time the subsequent swelling around the knee and attempt at draining the fire engine yellow synovial fluid failed. The attending physician told me about an orthopedic doctor who had a lot of success performing anterior cruciate reconstructions. The doctor's reputation resulted from the many successful operations he had conducted for all the athletes treated. Armed with that recommendation, I proceeded to the doctor's physician assistant, then on to the surgeon. They declared my anterior cruciate ligament wasted but claimed that the joint would strengthen with a barbaric operation.

The procedure started with an incision four inches below the kneecap on the outside of the leg and went upward to about three inches above the kneecap. The doctor cut a one-inch incision about six inches above the first. That smaller incision let the doctor cut a portion of the leg tendon. He then cut a lower portion of the tendon, removed it, and sutured it to the back of the knee. That procedure supposedly strengthened the knee from a failed anterior cruciate ligament. The doctor closed the large incision with a technique that left little scarring.

He laid a piece of wire in the incision and closed the gaping wound with a series of sutures. Pulling both ends of the wire tight left one-half inch of wire sticking out of my leg on each end. The operation took only three hours.

A cast, running from toes to crotch, stayed in place for four months so the graft could heal. After two months a small cut in the back part of the cast allowed minimal knee flexing of one inch.

The wire wounds itched when they began healing. Creativity took over when the itch couldn't be scratched. I crafted a straightened yet flexible coat hanger that reached from the top of the cast and satisfied my most important need.

After the doctor finally cut off the cast, he took hold of one end of the wire with a pair of pliers and said, "This is going to feel a little warm."

As he pulled the wire out, warmth came from my old friend friction. I enjoyed moving around without scooting on my butt. The least painful part of the procedure had ended, but now came time for rehab. I found it disconcerting watching my jelly-like calf muscle swing back and forth, because when a leg remained in a cast for that long muscles atrophied and needed strengthening.

Extended time in a cast also made the knee joint send a message to the body: "If you aren't going to use me, I'm going to lock in place with a set of false ligaments." Rehab was painful.

To have a full range of motion, those false ligaments needed busting loose. To understand the feeling, imagine a leg hanging over the edge of a curb while someone jumped on the suspended part, breaking it. The boring part of rehab occurred as the physician's assistant broke the false ligaments, one at a time. We repeated the process every week or so because sometimes the false ligaments re-formed if painful exercises didn't continue.

My preference for maximum pain all at once, after about two treatments, made me ask about breaking them all at the same time. The physician's assistant laughed and said, "Sure, if you think you can take it." He also said he wouldn't do it.

So I enlisted my old pal Ray. Ray was an old barhopping buddy. He always won drinking contests and never shied away from abusing his body, though it didn't show. I'm not sure if his immediate positive response to my request for help resulted from concern for me or his sadistic curiosity. We rehearsed on him.

While Ray, who had a thin, wiry physique, lay on his back, I took hold of his right ankle, lifted his leg to a forty-five-degree angle, and bent his knee to a ninety-degree angle. "Now be careful to push the ankle straight to the buttocks," I instructed. "That's important because if the motion varies to one side, it will ruin the entire procedure."

With me lying on my back and a piece of leather between my teeth, Ray started having second thoughts. It took only a little name-calling before my old pal came through. One downward motion produced multiple popping sounds as the scar tissue and nerve endings ripped apart. Ray laughed. "Damn, did you hear that?" I slowly rolled over on my side and kept from wetting myself. Later I paid the favor forward to another friend who became a fire chief not far from Wichita. He retired from that job and became a fire chief for a mountain resort community in Colorado.

When I returned to the physician's assistant, he saw the swelling. He said he didn't think I would do it, but everything seemed all right. As it turned out years later, the procedure eventually failed, and the knee joint needed replacing after retirement.

One small story about my knee joint replacement seems appropriate. Medical personnel performed a flawless procedure in phenomenal facilities near Denver, Colorado. Attending nurses, particularly Rachel and Linda, resembled angels.

After surgery, I looked at my menu choices for breakfast the next morning. The first choice, biscuits with gravy, completed my reading. That afternoon the hospital CEO came in and gave me his card. He told me if I needed anything to please let him know.

The surgical team catheterized me for a spinal block. That afternoon liquid flowed properly from the siphoning point to a water-retention container. In the early morning hours of the second day, a blockage must've occurred because my bladder messaged a sensation that I usually felt after a couple of beers.

One source of my pride had always been my bladder's capacity, but that pain exceeded my threshold. I pushed the sissy button.

The speaker came alive with the sound of someone's voice. "May I help you?"

"Something's wrong, and I need help."

The station nurse said, "Just a minute."

I didn't know if that meant attention within sixty seconds or placement on hold. I thought back to my disdain for those customer service phone messages that offered several options depending on one's needs. I always provided input when those organizations asked.

I asked them how they would like it if they called the fire department and received a voice message: "If you have a small fire, press one; if you have a medium-sized fire, press two; if you have a really big fire, press three; if you are experiencing a heart attack, press four." Then follow those choices with a complete set of secondary questions for each of those categories.

While I was going over my quality control thoughts for organizations, Rachel flew in and folded her wings. She immediately recognized the problem but needed permission before irrigating the catheter intake. That took so long and the pressure was so excruciating that I contemplated pulling the device out. Rachel explained why that wouldn't be a good idea. She said, "The inflatable intake device won't come out without grave consequences."

Since the discussion focused on the inner workings of my favorite body part, common sense prevailed. Rachel eventually brought a critical care nurse, and they injected some air into the intake tube. Over one thousand cubic centimeters of fluid exited immediately. The real problem happened the next day.

The on-duty doctor who came in the next morning knew of my desire for immediate removal of the torture device. His words stunned me. "It would be better if the device remained in place for a few days because there's a chance of a stroke or heart attack if we remove it now."

At that point in my life, I controlled the outward appearance of rapidly growing dissatisfaction with what I heard. The heart monitor ratted me out. The doctor looked up, saw the increased heart rate, and asked, "Are you okay?"

"I'm not okay because I live four hours away, over the Continental Divide, where there are no urologists. I have full use of my lower extremities and don't need the device. Where were you last night? Additionally, if I have a heart attack or stroke, I'm not far from one of the best level-one trauma centers in the state. That's where I would be airlifted to, once we wasted precious time and money." Because of heavy medication, I don't think I ended with my usual comment that if I did my job the way he did his, two communities would have burned to the ground, but I'm not sure. They soon removed the device.

I remembered the CEO's card, sent him a letter, and asked that he please commend Rachel and Linda. I praised him on their mission statement, service, and facilities. I suggested he refer the bladder matter to a physician's review committee for quality control but never heard back from him. My hope was that no other patient would have to go through an ordeal like mine.

I thought back to the time as fire chief when I encouraged fire officers to keep occupants informed about what we did during fire operations. Tell them why we just chopped a hole in their roof or intentionally broke a window for ventilation and how those actions will produce a better outcome in the end. Tell them we chopped a hole in Sheetrock after the fire to find any hidden fire potential. Tell them we sifted through and put piles of debris outside in a rough cleanup to avoid a rekindle. Ask if they need the Red Cross and suggest they contact their insurance agent. That's part of customer service during and after a fire operation. When customers experience traumatizing events, that's when they most need answers, reassurance, and help.

17

A Change Is Coming

At the end of 1979 and the beginning of 1980, the economy made for some character-building times. Interest rates soared into the teens. The one thing politicians did that gave an appearance of helping the economy was cut government spending. The Wichita city manager at the time, Gene Denton, foresaw what was coming, so he had all city department heads write a paper on the challenges facing their departments in that decade. Since my class teaching assignments included that subject, I asked the fire chief if he wanted me to pen something for his review, and he said he would appreciate it. The chief made a few changes and forwarded the document to the city manager. Not long after, the fire chief announced his retirement. He supported higher education for firefighters and was the deputy chief of operations when we secured the fire science degree program. The chief certainly earned every bit of his pay and deserved a peaceful retirement. He shepherded the Wichita Fire Department through its lowest point in history with the strike in 1978 and always concerned himself with firefighter safety. He was the chief who introduced lime-yellow fire trucks to the WFD.

If changing a fire truck's color doesn't sound like much, try it in any community. It doesn't matter that lime yellow is the most visible color in the spectrum. It also doesn't matter that the human eye picks up that color in its peripheral vision more quickly than red. It also doesn't matter that school crosswalk signs and safety vests use that color.

Just yesterday I asked an old colleague if he could find the study that an eye doctor produced with empirical evidence of that color's value. In the e-mail back came the name of a department that tried it twenty-five years ago and then stopped because they found the public recognized red fire trucks better because of familiarity. I enjoyed seeing how that resistance to change with no countering scientific evidence remained alive and well in the fire service.

The chief also ordered all firefighters off the tailboard and into seats behind the truck's cab. Not long afterward a fire truck rollover accident occurred at Twenty-First Street and Oliver, which would have been a disaster had firefighters been riding the tailboard.

Finally, that chief led the way in using new technology for locating fire stations. Wichita teamed up with IBM and Public Technology Incorporated and became the first community that used computer modeling to locate facilities. That legacy, although with different software, lives on today. Because of that chief, Floyd Hobbs, and fire chiefs that preceded him, I inherited a great department.

I responded to a Wichita fire chief recruitment notice in *Fire Command* magazine and hand-delivered a February 20, 1980, letter to the personnel director. The letter included an outline of my fire command experience, administrative background, education, and teaching achievements. My administrative and leadership accomplishments representing the union—previously criticized— now became a benefit. The letter ended with a pledge to pursue our top goals of fire prevention, efficient and effective fire suppression, and an expanding role in emergency medical services.

After a nationwide search and initial screening, personnel narrowed the candidates to seventeen and scheduled them for pre-assessment interviews on Friday, May 16, 1980. The deputy city manager and director of water, both well-respected administrators, conducted those interviews.

On May 19, they narrowed internal candidates to nine, and along with three external candidates, all reported for an assessment center process on May 28 and 29. The assessment process came to prominence in the military because of a need for quickly evaluating thousands of officer candidates when the country had geared up for World War II.

This process subjected each fire chief candidate to a series of exercises. One exercise provided a stack of communications found in a typical in-basket. That exercise measured how a candidate prioritized and handled each item. Another exercise, group interaction, measured leadership and consensus building. Each candidate had a profile of different department members, but the group could only send one member to a special seminar. The stated goal: get the group to send your member. My profiled member was overall below average. I listened as the competitive juices kicked in and candidates fought for their profiled members. I finally laughed and said, "You know, I don't think my member is the best and brightest, so let's go around the table and read out loud each profile. Then we can decide as a group which member should attend the seminar for the betterment of the organization." That's what the true leadership and consensus exercise was all about—not competition. As it turned out, all profiled members were below average.

A panel interview on relevant organizational topics measured responses and communication skills. One panel member asked what candidates thought about attracting more minority candidates. I found out later that many candidates passively answered that the hiring process was open to all individuals. I pledged my support for attracting more diversification in the workforce. I went beyond support by outlining the IAFF program we implemented when I was union president that attracted minority candidates.

All the exercises measured how a candidate would perform in the position of fire chief. Dr. John Belt of the WSU School of Business developed all the exercises and oversaw the process. Teams of trained assessors graded all exercises. Each evaluation team consisted of a businessperson in the community, a technical expert, and a trained team-leader assessor from the School of Business at WSU. The team leaders guaranteed documented behavioral performances, thereby eliminating undocumented grading. The business members provided community input and authoritative witnesses to a professional process. The technical experts included fire chiefs from Dallas, Denver, Des Moines, Milwaukee, and Tucson.

After the assessment, finalists included three inside candidates and two outside candidates, who each reported for a one-on-one interview with the city manager. Afterward, the personnel director called each finalist. He called me the day after all interviews. "I will call the ones not selected. The city manager's secretary will call the anointed one for a brief meeting and a scheduled press conference."

"No offense, but I don't want to hear from you again."

He laughed. "Okay."

On the morning of June 4, 1980, the city manager's secretary called. "The manager wants to meet you somewhere on the east side of the city for lunch. Where would you suggest?" My pulse quickened as I tried concealing my delight. I quickly thought of an upscale place, where a good friend of mine was a member.

"How about the Candle Club?"

"I know he's been there before so that should be fine."

Then I called my friend and he happily made a reservation with my promise to call him afterward. I kept thinking, *This is happening*. When time allowed, I needed to reevaluate the implications both personally and professionally.

I arrived at the Candle Club in eastern Wichita about 11:45 a.m., fifteen minutes before our scheduled noon meeting. The low-level starburst ceiling lighting looked like something out of the late 1950s. Club members appeared to me as a group of older folks, who talked in subdued conversations. The overall atmosphere seemed consistent with my image of a supper club, not at all like the clubs I frequented.

Then Gene Denton, the city manager, walked in, and I stood, shook his hand, and greeted him. We sat down. "I wanted to visit with you before the news conference this afternoon." His first question was blunt and to the point. "Is there anything in your past that could come out later that might be embarrassing?"

"Yes, but nothing criminal." The corners of his mouth turned upward, and his wide smile revealed brightly polished teeth. I saw the laugh wrinkles around his eyes. He rearranged his silverware to one side, ordered a glass of sparkling water from the waitress who just stopped at the table, and told her he wouldn't be ordering any food. "I need to go by my home, then back to city hall for a news conference," he said as he smiled at me. I ordered a glass of unsweetened iced tea. The manager pushed the butter and rolls to one side as well. "I never use butter. It's pure fat." We quickly got down to business.

"I realize that promoting you from lieutenant over the ranks of captain, district chief, fire marshal, and deputy chiefs will be difficult for some people to understand. Those people will also have difficulty accepting a thirty-three-year-old chief who only has thirteen years of service. You are responsible for your continued success, but my initial decision came from four main factors:

1. Demonstrated leadership among the rank and file;
2. Demonstrated dedication to professionalism of the firefighting service indicated by personal achievements in graduate and

postgraduate education, as well as taking a founding role and lecturer position in fire science courses at Wichita State University;

3. Demonstrated a willingness to innovate, both regarding fire technology and management, as well as a high sense of public service in support of emergency medical training for fire personnel;

4. Expressed commitment to strong management and organizational discipline."

The manager then listed a series of challenges the department would face, including budgetary constraints and innovative ways of coping with those challenges. He found out that I'd helped the recently retired fire chief with the paper titled 'The Challenges Facing the Fire Service in the 1980s." That paper, coupled with the areas above, provided the basis for his decision.

The same process had selected a police chief. That chief, Richard LaMunyon, a young captain, was promoted over several ranks, and the press nicknamed him the "Boy Chief." They nicknamed me the "Baby Chief." I know beyond all doubt that if Richard hadn't been successful, I wouldn't have received an opportunity, either. Richard later retired and became a city administrator for Maize, Kansas, near Wichita.

No doubt the excellence in police services he instilled carried forward to an outstanding department. Several WPD officers became police chiefs, private security managers, and sheriffs. Richard and I collaborated on several projects, including interdepartmental sports competition fundraisers and a joint facility located near US 54 and Edgemoor.

The press conference took place in the city hall meeting room. Gene Denton, as usual, did all the talking. His smooth and steady voice matched his suave and sophisticated manner as he recalled the selection process. Members of the television, radio, and print media all looked a little stunned. I knew many of them, but as one reporter later told me, "I can't believe the city manager had the bravery to make that decision." After the press conference, I went upstairs and met with the deputy chiefs of operations and administration, as well as the fire marshal. The deputy chief of administration had decided to retire if not selected as fire chief. He provided excellent professional service and a loyal department commitment.

The deputy chief of operations acted in an interim capacity, and I later interviewed him along with others before recommending him for promotion. I interviewed other candidates for the position, thereby gaining different points of view, and brought overall support to the one promoted because he competed. That operations deputy became the absolute face of leadership and loyalty. It was easy being loyal to people that everyone liked and whose policies they approved of. He's the poor fellow who caught all the slings and arrows with his bare hands because he became the intermediary between the old and new guard. He remains active with the retired firefighters' association. His name is Walt Campbell.

I then interviewed candidates for the deputy chief of administration position. I recommended the office and records district chief for promotion to the position of administrative deputy and a captain to his position. Both those men had been candidates for the chief's position. People who filled areas of my weakness and inexperience became important to me.

About that time, I developed three expectations for every promoted officer. The first expectation focused on training because that was their single most important non-emergency activity. Fire departments trained every day in some form because unusual emergencies didn't happen every day, but firefighters had to handle all types of calls. Company officers knew the training needs of their subordinates better than anyone else. If we held company officers responsible for how their crews performed, they should provide the basic in-service training necessary before the emergency occurred. We shifted the training division from providing basic in-service training to specialized training and overall monitoring compliance with emergency operating policies and procedures. More training became the first recommendation after every accident (mistake).

My second expectation focused on discipline. By "discipline" I meant the positive kind where minds become disciplined through study material and bodies become disciplined through being fit to handle job stress. If negative disciplinary action became necessary, I pledged my support.

My final expectation involved loyalty, not to a person, but to the fire chief rank that recommended them for promotion. In return, they could question any policy or directive before implementation— but not afterward in the field. That affected morale. If they had any negative comments after implementation, I invited them to come in anytime and roll around on the floor, kick, and bitch. Once a policy was decided, however, they better support it or serious consequences would follow. I only provided those serious consequences a couple of times. Most officers held in high regard the three basics: training, discipline, and loyalty.

I traveled back to Wichita in 2012 and spoke at an awards ceremony, where I noticed a large emblem outside the new training facility. Around the emblem's edge were the words "Training, discipline, and education." Firefighters took qualities we worked for much further as I tried doing what my city manager had instilled in me.

The city manager, one of those kucimags mentioned earlier, spoke softly and often. He appointed department heads that strongly advocated for their professions. He embodied confidence and saw no department head as a threat. He defined public service as an academician and practitioner of excellence in government service.

From my initial hiring to retirement, I worked in varying capacities for seven different city managers, and E. H. "Gene" Denton topped them all. After Gene left Wichita, he became a county manager for Johnson County, Kansas, near KU, and the home of those kucimags. He remained active in the International City/County Management Association (ICMA). When I told him, he enjoyed the story of the old union boss who said ICMA stood for "I can't manage anything."

Division chief Bruce Roberts and I made him a round conference table of oak for his office. Bruce did most of the work, and that's why his name appeared first on the dedication plaque. We used walnut to inlay the circle and enclosed square, with the ICMA logo. Gene was so proud of that table he insisted on a picture with him seated at the table and Roberts and me standing behind him. Of course, I wore something pink and will explain why later. That table was the only thing Gene requested when he left Wichita, and some politician wouldn't give it to him.

I recently learned that someone rescued the table from a scrap heap and returned it to the fire department, where it rightfully resides today. The department is committed to the ICMA tradition of excellence in public service.

Gene wanted a change agent, and he got one. I provided him with a memo at the end of my first year as chief. Typically, five to seven goals and objectives received consideration for accomplishment and evaluation. I submitted those seven and an addendum with thirty more. My strategy of change concentrated on health and safety, fire prevention, better emergency medical service delivery, and overall efficiency.

Three years later we compiled a list of all significant changes. The total: 145. Number eighty-two, the toilet paper change from squares to rolls, became our finest moment, according to Loudy. That change became one of the many things we did to boost morale. I wrongly thought that significant increases in productivity would stave off across-the-board politically motivated budget cuts. Many differences separated public from private sectors and fostered mediocrity. Where's the incentive to excel if politicians treat all departments the same?

Also, people originally huddled together in masses for public safety and that should take precedence over parks and recreation. It didn't take long before I began looking at the overall importance of different community amenities. Gene sent me a survey that the ICMA produced. The survey ranked citizens' concerns in order of importance. Gene pointed out the top concerns before police and fire services. Water and sewer, transportation, smooth roads, and recreational opportunities led the list. Gene grinned as he handed me the survey. "Now, don't feel bad. These services are what people use every day. Thanks to your fire prevention efforts, citizens don't use your services that much. But stay after that EMS transport system." I smiled back at his gentle instructional effort, always rooted in the ICMA professional tradition.

Gene passed away a few years back, and I found out over a year afterward. The master's ring I mentioned earlier didn't have my birthstone color as my undergraduate ring did. Rather, it had a black insert like Gene's. When I wear a watch, the face has the International Association of Fire Chiefs logo, a symbol of excellence in public service. I'm a lifetime member.

After my promotion to chief, some personnel doubted my ability to still pick up a horse. Bubba, or as I called him, "Pink," sauntered through the administrative offices one day. To understand his nickname Pink, one had to have known his real first name. His full name is Floyd Bess. I called for a camera.

Pink on Top

I.C.M.A. Table

18

SAFETY FIRST, LAST, ALWAYS

The deputy chief of administration I recommended for promotion, Floyd Crawford, was a candidate for fire chief. As the officer in charge of office and records, Floyd developed every budget since the 1960s and served three fire chiefs before my appointment. Providing strength for my weak area of budget development and number crunching, Floyd became my green shade.

Floyd often said that taxpayer dollars didn't belong to us. Therefore, we needed diligence in how we used them, even after allocation. As the officer in charge of accounts payable, he had pored over utility bills for every fire station. If something looked out of order, he called the district chief and station captain and found reasons for the variance. His scrutiny of numbers led to the discovery of gas and water leaks. He also found billing mistakes, investigated the reasons, and sought resolutions. His ledger books dated back years.

One time the phone company notified Floyd that the phone bill had not been paid for Fire Station No. 4, and the phone would soon be disconnected. Floyd informed them that the city paid the phone bill, and he could prove it. He told them, "Sit still, I will be right there." He grabbed his armload of ledger books and proceeded to the phone company's office. When he arrived, he asked how far back their records went. They replied one year. Floyd said his went back to the original installation of the phone. Floyd opened his ledger and provided a purchase order and requisition number demonstrating payment.

Floyd said, "You did cash the check."

Floyd solved the problem because the city paid all fire department phone bills with one check. Three years later the same thing happened again, and Floyd reminded them of the last time when he went to their office. Now they had to come to his office. He told them that he and his ledger books would be waiting. After his second tutorial, that never happened again on his watch. That's the kind of attention to detail and concern for taxpayer dollars the department provided for years.

Floyd was in his late fifties and weighed about 160 pounds. Although he had a lean muscular look, he didn't work out until we started our fitness program. We usually met at city hall around 5:30 a.m. Police chief LaMunyon had a little exercise area with showers and lockers for himself and his subordinates. He permitted our use of the facility. We did our flexibility and strength exercises, then went outside for a two-mile run. Floyd had no trouble with the program. When older firefighters complained about the fitness program, I just pointed to Floyd.

Floyd's distinguishing feat was his ability to stand an overturned wooden Douglas chair. The chair had lathe-turned legs, curved back support, and an oval-carved handle hole on its back support. He accomplished this feat by getting down on his hands and knees next to the overturned chair and gripping the back leg about four inches above the bottom. Then, in one motion, he flexed his wrist toward his elbow, thereby standing the chair upright.

One day a rookie, an ex-marine weighing about 240 pounds, participated in a typical indoctrination process. As the rookie tried and failed at standing the chair, a voice sounded over the fire station speakers, requesting Floyd's presence upstairs. He climbed the stairs and there laid two chairs on their backs. Floyd got down on his hands and knees and instantly set both chairs upright. As Floyd left, the rookie firefighter asked how he did that. Floyd replied, "It's not strength, young man. It's all willpower."

Floyd did one more thing the big boys couldn't. I witnessed it one day when we visited old Station 2. Floyd demonstrated the flagpole display, an exhibition of strength and will. The pole, of course, was the same one I had used.

Floyd accomplished the display by taking hold of the four-inch-diameter pole at the knee level with his hand pointing downward and arm straight. With a jump he grabbed the pole above his head with his other hand, then kept his legs rigid and straight out, resembling a flag. Like me, many tried and failed to replicate that feat.

My best effort began by placing my elbow against my stomach and then grabbing the pole at the knee level with my hand pointing down. The other hand grabbed the pole above my head, but all leverage pivoted from my lower elbow against my body. That's called cheating. The mental health PhD in my early psychological interview would have been proud. He probably would've said something about the symbolism with the poles as well.

If I worried over some issue and it involved Floyd's area of responsibility, he always said, "Only one person at a time should worry over something, so let me do that." He added, "Now if you want to, I won't."

I later modified that bit of wisdom: "Only one person at a time should worry over something, and that person should be the one who can do something about it."

Floyd also told me stories about my predecessors. I particularly enjoyed stories about Chief McGaughey, who died in a previously mentioned fire. He had quite a temper and displayed his displeasure by pounding on his desk. When his temper reached its height, the force of his blow sent the phone receiver on his desk flying from its cradle. My favorite story involved the time he had difficulty getting city hall to replace a dilapidated and dangerous aerial ladder. The chief finally told them they would soon see the ladder permanently parked in front of city hall for them to explain. They replaced the ladder truck.

Floyd taught me to respect certain traditions and the efforts of those before me as I fulfilled my change agent role. Floyd, like Deputy Chief Campbell, supported my strategy of change concerning firefighter health and safety. The tactical support for that strategy included physical fitness and fire prevention, in addition to efficient and effective service delivery. Physical fitness and the appointment of a safety/fitness officer were two important initiatives. A leading cause of line-of-duty deaths among firefighters is heart attacks. My research found that only physical fitness prepared a body for handling the rigors of firefighting.

In 1978, two years before becoming chief, I took a college class on organizational conflict and stress. I knew something about individual stress and fighting fire. Studies were conducted using portable heart monitors that recorded heart rates during alarm response and actual firefighting operations. During sleep, resting heart rates during the "readiness to serve posture" measured in the 60–70 beats per minute range, depending on an individual's fitness.

When an alarm sounded, heart monitors recorded that firefighters' heart rates per minute instantly soared to 100 or more. During firefighting, heart rates sometimes measured above 175 beats per minute, which exceeded the maximum range for strenuous exercise. The anticipatory reaction of the unknown and extreme temperature changes, coupled with the actual physical rigors and lack of warm-up exercises, caused excessive heart rates.

No athlete in the world begins without stretching and warm-up exercises, let alone attempting anything from a full resting position. The best way a body coped with stressors was with a good fitness regimen. Later, we dropped one tiny bombshell on some firefighters for their own good.

As the physical fitness program progressed, we added different elements. From the beginning, firefighters kept track of their weight, resting and exercise heart rates, as well as their performance in the categories of endurance, strength, and flexibility.

We began endurance exercises with walking and progressed to a benchmark of running one and a half miles in twelve minutes. All firefighters saw progress with improvements in their resting and exercise heart rates. The strength exercises provided their own documented improvements. The flexibility and stretching exercises prepared firefighters for running, and strength exercises and provided a category for me to excel in. I have always been physically flexible. To this day, I can stand straight-legged and place my palms on the floor behind my feet. I can still do the splits, although it takes a little longer now at positioning in a final pose.

One year into the fitness program, some younger firefighters took an informal and nonscientific survey regarding improvement in firefighters' sex lives. Some men said no, but wives and girlfriends said yes.

We purchased weight-lifting equipment from defunct gymnasiums and spread that equipment among fire stations. We provided stationary bicycles with a regimen that produced the metabolic equivalent of the 1.5-mile run for folks who couldn't run for various reasons. We also provided nutritional information and hired a firefighter who was a yoga instructor. Those yoga routines became entertaining.

The time for that tiny bombshell had arrived. The percentage of firefighters who smoked was similar to the general population of smokers with military service. About 30 percent of our universe smoked. Firefighters had a "heart and lung clause" in their retirement benefits package. Our clause stated that firefighters who contracted a heart or lung ailment automatically received 75 percent of their salary for the rest of their lives. Firefighters deserved that necessary and presumptive clause because of the job's nature.

Although 30 percent of the department smoked, 75 percent of those who left the job with a heart or lung ailment were smokers. Smokers, as a group, also disproportionately used higher amounts of sick and injury leave. We took action to protect the heart and lung clause. We began by banning smoking in fire stations and fire department offices. It took a few years before the rest of city hall and the private sector caught up. Next, we developed a signed contract for all new employees that provided they would not smoke tobacco products as a condition of employment. If caught smoking, they were automatically fired. The city attorney helped with the legal contractual language.

In 1987 less than 12 percent of fire department employees still smoked. One time I asked Dr. Paul O. Davis, who helped develop the combat challenge games for firefighters, this question: If he could mandate either a nonsmoking policy or a physical fitness policy for firefighters, which would he choose? He answered unequivocally. "No smoking." Paul remains the foremost authority on firefighter physical fitness.

The idea of contractual nonsmoking agreements for new hires came from Charley Rule, a fire chief in Alexandria, Virginia, and a longtime friend of mine. I still remember him telling me that it wouldn't work in a major city.

Charley Rule was the biggest agitator I ever met. A professional journal article asked, "What would the perfect firefighter be like?" Without hesitation, Charley noted, "The perfect firefighter combined East Coast aggressiveness and West Coast innovation with the integrity of Midwest firefighters."

That one statement made all firefighters in the country equally angry because it meant they weren't part of the other two groups. I hadn't heard such an outcry since I ran through the television room when a John Wayne movie played, proclaiming, "Clint Eastwood can whip John Wayne's butt any day of the week." That run included a speed slide down the pole to a hiding place downstairs. Agitation with Charley's comment didn't remain local. It spread nationwide.

The only person who ever got to Charley was Al Conner, a secretary for the International Association of Fire Chiefs. He and Charley roomed together one night, in separate beds. Charley stayed up late, no doubt, at a nearby Irish pub discussing the Troubles. During Charley's absence, Al went down to the chef and slipped him a twenty for an uncooked crab. Al placed it in Charley's bed. Late that night when Charley came in and climbed into bed, the commotion began.

Charley climbed out of bed and groped along the wall until he found a light switch. The lights came on, and one-vowel words in two-word sentences began flowing. Al climbed out of bed and walked over to Charley's. "That's the worst case of crabs I've ever seen," Al said. "Charley, you should probably seek medical attention."

Charley deserved that last comment because he used to call some of his fire chief pals when he knew they were absent. When their secretaries informed Charley of a chief's absence, he said, "I'm Dr. Smith, and I have the results of his recent lab tests from the health department. That's okay; tell him I'll call back later," then he disconnected the phone.

Remember the caution about aerial ladders tipping over if the driver didn't deploy the outriggers? Al had an experience with that kind of accident (mistake). Charley probably brought that old story up again, which triggered the prank. Retaliation knew few boundaries. During all our pranking and sometimes arguments, one principle always prevailed: firefighter safety first, last, always!

19

SAFETY, A MATTER OF LUCK?

Fire prevention became another component of our safety campaign. Naturally, if we prevented a fire, no danger existed for our firefighters. I inherited a premier fire prevention program. The fire marshal was a finalist for fire chief. He and the others who worked for him provided that excellent component of our service delivery. The fire marshal's qualifications and performance led him to a job with the Department of State after he retired. I provided a recommendation to the FBI for his security clearance.

After the fire marshal retired, I recommended the executive officer for promotion to fire marshal because of his education, research, and development duties, and of course, because he had been a candidate for fire chief. Jim Cloud spent time on another shift at Station 10 and pursued his college education. Jim retired after I did, then became chief of a model fire department he built in Westminster, Colorado.

We focused on three components in our fire prevention program: public education, code enforcement, and investigation. I strengthened those programs through a series of goals and objectives. Fire prevention should always be the primary goal of any department.

My favorite prevention poster hung in the prevention offices. It pictured a firefighter, battle-worn, with roaring flames in the background. The caption read, "There's no glory in fighting a fire that could have been prevented."

Wow! That pissed off the suppression firefighters. More than one came into my office and complained. I always responded the same way: "When you fully consider the premise, isn't it true? I believe prevention should be your primary goal as well."

About 1982 we undertook one noteworthy fire prevention initiative. The mandatory smoke detector city ordinance required smoke detectors for all triplex and larger properties. We offered free smoke detectors for low-income and disabled individuals. Fire marshal Jim Cloud and public education specialist Jim Harris successfully managed the smoke detector program, which resulted in fewer fire fatalities than in previous years.

The International Brotherhood of Electrical Workers donated their services for the installation of smoke detectors for folks with special needs. I hadn't given much thought about the needs of hearing-impaired people until receiving a request from Leon Vanetta, who wanted me to visit his and his wife's home to discuss their needs. Even though the mandatory smoke detector ordinance didn't apply to Leon's situation, it impressed me that our smoke detector public education efforts drew attention from different constituencies.

I went to Leon's home, and he and his wife educated me. They wanted the fire chief to understand their needs, as well as those of others who had hearing impairments. Leon pointed to his smoke detector and in his labored language said, "Go ahead and push the button. You will hear it, but I won't."

Jim Harris worked with Leon and his wife and found a strobe light smoke detector. Leon wanted to make sure the strobe light detector would be acceptable. I answered, "Of course." Leon assured me that he would use both detectors in case they had non-hearing-impaired visitors.

I agreed to visiting requests like Leon's because of a fire fatality that occurred in eastern Wichita. I responded to large fires, incidents involving firefighter injuries, and all fires involving fatalities. In one incident a young mother died from smoke inhalation, leaving a toddler without his mother. The rental apartment had no smoke detector. I had seen several fire fatalities before, but because of my single-parent status with a young son, that one got to me. My sorrow for the toddler son needed a cathartic symbol of action.

At the scene I found a Polaroid picture of a beautiful young mother with her son. Her father let me keep that photo as a reminder to consider initiatives, like the smoke detector ordinance, that prevented such tragic occurrences. I kept that picture in my upper-right-hand desk drawer for the remainder of my tenure as fire chief.

Another major effort concentrated on upgrading our emergency medical service (EMS) capabilities, which I promised the city manager

Gene Denton we would do. I had spent time in the mid-1970s as the union president working with Charles Duncan, a television journalist, on an exposé of the then-private ambulance service. Those stories led to the political decision that made the ambulance service a county government operation. Politicians reacted more quickly to news stories than staff suggestions. My original goal in the 1970s was consolidation with the transport system and the fire department. Since I didn't hold a position of authority, I couldn't fight to make EMS part of the fire department. The local medical society and health department filled that leadership void. They supported a countywide operation.

Once I was promoted to fire chief, it became a priority to try for consolidation. We began upgrading our medical services by hiring a registered nurse, Marilyn Crowley, who provided our emergency medical technician recertification and mobile intensive care technician capabilities.

We intended to consolidate with EMS, a county operation, thereby maximizing both departments' productivity. That consolidated service delivery model developed as a result of medics who came out of the Vietnam War and joined fire departments. In addition to being from a desirable military pool, those veterans had emergency medical field training and experience. Before that consolidated model, most fire departments only provided first aid. We fully prepared for consolidation when politicians scuttled the program, so we built a model first responder program instead. Those politicians didn't show any interest in increased productivity and revenue generation but had no problem with personnel reductions. The most forceful case against the consolidation came in whispers to city council members: "What if firefighters go on strike again, and they also run the ambulance service?" When the merger with county EMS and the WFD collapsed, the EMS transport system remained a county-run quality operation, although it was more expensive than consolidation.

In the mid-1980s, we started a medically related program called Respond Early and Control Hypertension (REACH). That program became part of an overall strategy that increased productivity and provided more community outreach. For too long firefighters stayed behind closed doors, leaving a public that relied on old stereotypes for firefighters. The REACH program let citizens go to any fire station on Saturday between 10:00 a.m. and 2:00 p.m. for free blood pressure checks. We monitored the program, and it became so successful that we received an award from the local medical society. People seemed more at ease with firefighters than medical staff because of the "white coat syndrome." The white lab coats of medical personnel made patients' blood pressure artificially rise.

The REACH program kept our skill levels of blood pressure testing more accurate because of more practice. The program also motivated firefighters to monitor their own blood pressure. Marilyn Crowley led that program and others. She had a real knack for handling training sessions for our firefighters. They called her "the drill sergeant." She had a way with teaching firefighters how to think. I remember a tutorial she gave on communicable diseases. Marilyn summed it up by saying, "If it's wet and it isn't yours, protect yourself."

As first responders, we began responding to all medical calls, which significantly increased our productivity regarding call volume. Medically related calls accounted for over 70 percent of our total call volume. We purchased quick response vehicles (QRVs) that were heavy-duty pickups with small water tanks for field firefighting and assisting with car wrecks, and also carried equipment for medical calls. The QRVs lessened the workload on expensive pumpers and left the pumpers in service for answering other calls. The two QRV firefighters could also join in with a ladder or pumper company, thereby properly staffing those companies to four or five personnel for structural firefighting responses.

In 1985 we reviewed all our past efforts that ensured firefighter health and safety. Those safety efforts concentrated on the following areas, which established a culture of safety by:
- maintaining a good health and physical fitness program;
- managing a comprehensive prevention program;
- developing and monitoring a comprehensive training program;
- developing, training, and enforcing policies and procedures such as an incident command system;
- maintaining a prefire planning program; and
- providing the best equipment available.

I've consulted with many fire department chiefs who claimed they did all of the above, but when auditing training records and reviewing policies, procedures, and prefire plans, I found no such documentation. Prefire plans had a drawing of a building that included all the information a commander needed to consider if a building were on fire. People asked me years later if luck had anything to do with the fact that no firefighter was mortally wounded under my command. I always smiled and said no.

20

MANAGING CHAOS

The first multiple-alarm fire after I was appointed chief occurred at the old city hall because lightning struck the clock tower on top of the building. (By the way, lightning causes the only accidental fires, period! Three things cause all other fires: men, women, and children. I welcome any debate to the contrary.)

As I later described to the media, the fire-ground operation at old city hall was absolutely textbook. It helped that the fire burned through the top of the tower, and smoke vented. An extended aerial ladder doused burning embers falling on the roof below. A picture showed Maxi the firefighter working on top of the extended ladder.

The interior-attack operation featured a hose line (also seen in the picture) used to extinguish the tower fire from inside. Simultaneously a ladder company spread tarps from the interior tower entrance down around the stairwell and into an elevator shaft. Water fell back from the tower onto tarps, then channeled to the elevator shaft. Firefighters then pumped water out of the shaft. That operation avoided internal water damage. I inherited a great department.

My former shift and crew from Station 2 handled the operation. I knew they could take care of firefighting operations, but wondered if they still had the same fun. I soon found out that fire station life proceeded just fine without me.

Remember Loudy? He thought that rolled toilet paper marked our most magnificent change. Loudy used the same coping mechanism I did during difficult times by applying contemporary expressions to tragic events. For instance, unrecognizable burned bodies became

Photo: WFD Staff

Old City Hall Fire

"crispy critters." Dehumanizing gruesome remains let us cope long enough to get the job done and sublimate personal feelings for later reflection. On one incident while assigned to Station 2, Loudy and I responded to an unresponsive patient, and despite all our efforts, we couldn't revive him. I broke the silence heading back to the fire station by changing some popular song's words and applying them to our situation. Dark humor helped us cope with more serious thoughts of witnessing life slipping away. We also blocked thoughts of just what had happened in this person's life that brought him to homelessness.

Loudy also expressed sick humor in written form. He sat in the watchman's booth and wrote short stories. None of those stories were publishable. I doubt the ACLU would have defended his free speech rights.

One day, while sitting in my office, I received my favorite Loudy writing. Deputy Chief Campbell came in with a letter that described how one of our radios was lost. At the time we still had a few antiquated portable radios that resembled small suitcases with long cords and microphones attached. Loudy and his co-worker had finished an inspection of some property, and no doubt began discussing the importance of fire prevention. They placed the radio on a side running board of the fire truck. The discussion became lengthy, and they didn't hear the radio's cries for help as they drove off.

Someone found the radio and enjoyed announcing their presence until the battery died. Loudy, as the officer in charge, had to write a letter outlining what occurred and explain what corrective actions would ensure that it wouldn't happen again. That procedure was always required.

Loudy had some time on his hands, so he wrote two letters. One letter complied with tradition. The other letter criticized the older-style radios, the radio's complicity in the unfortunate occurrence, and the ridiculous need for writing these letters. The letter ended with a declaratory statement that if we didn't like his letter, we could mark an *X* on his butt and either take a bite or kiss that spot.

The only mistake he made was showing that second letter to his co-workers, one of whom got into his locker, and sent it to the fire chief through the proper channels. Deputy Chief Campbell didn't share my amusement. I remembered telling employees to question traditions, be creative, and offer new suggestions. I didn't want any of that stifled. It's a whole lot easier to slow people down than make them giddyup.

We finally settled on bringing him downtown for a counseling session. I can only imagine the humility that overcame that budding writer on his slow journey to headquarters. My sitting in on the counseling session was out of the question because of my inability to keep a straight face. I'm reasonably sure Loudy's pal, LJ, had dispatched the letter.

Loudy, or Jerry Lowderman, moved to Arkansas after retirement and worked as a teller for a local bank. He left physical fitness far behind and, at one report, weighed over three hundred pounds. He billed himself as the largest banker in Arkansas.

Firefighters such as Loudy and others performed good tactical operations at fire scenes like the one at old city hall. Good firefighting skills began with basic training and continued with all in-service training. For years chief officers received promotions because of their tactical firefighting skills. Successful command of strategy that coordinated tactical skills, though, was gained through trial-and-error experience without formal guidelines. That was about to change with the introduction of the incident command system (ICS).

That was a major initiative of ours. Simply stated, ICS provides an orderly method for managing chaos. In any major emergency, the first arriving unit takes command and initiates a strategy. That strategy involves a plan of action. Tactics such as ventilation, extinguishment, and rescue support a plan of action.

A larger emergency operation requires more tactical operations than a smaller one. Communication is key to coordinating individual operations. Each tactical action needs communication to the incident commander, who has the ultimate responsibility for overall strategy. The orchestration of many tactical operations precisely implemented, supporting a good strategy, has the best chance of good results. The best commanders also know when to give up, provide containment, and let it burn. I saw heroic firefighting efforts resulting in unbelievable fire stops, then watched an insurance company approve a total demolition.

Firefighter deaths that don't occur, like fires prevented, can't be accurately measured. Except for heart attacks, firefighter deaths that do occur usually can be traced back to actions taken without a commander's knowledge, which is called freelancing, or by bad assignments from a commander. Those bad assignments usually stem from a lack of information on prefire plans, lack of information from fire companies, or inexperienced fire personnel untrained in ICS use.

All the what-to-think processes together cannot overcome an ICS commander who has judgment issues that result from how-to-think difficulties.

Previous to ICS, some fire chiefs had a lot of knowledge and experience, and some did not. Although no substitute for experience, ICS provided a format for managing all emergencies effectively. Our fitness officer also acted as a safety officer at emergency scenes. That began a key component for the introduction of ICS. A safety officer becomes the eyes and ears for command by constantly monitoring all fire operations for safety considerations.

In 1979, the year before my fire chief promotion, the WFD lost ten people to budget cuts. Budget reductions were mandated to pay for the negotiated pay raises after the strike. Politicians needed something, however, to disguise the retaliatory nature of the personnel reductions. As mentioned early on, the fire department had three districts and three shifts. The nine district chiefs on three shifts had drivers for the chiefs. Many referred to the drivers as chief's aides, or worst of all, chauffeurs. Drivers could concentrate on emergency driving while district chiefs concentrated on formulating a strategy or plan of action before arrival on scene. That plan of action included referencing prefire plans for a structure involved in a fire.

At a scene, a driver aided a district chief by keeping track of different considerations like the position of various companies and their task assignments during a large-scale operation. A driver also gained valuable experience by observing the command of emergency operations. None of that mattered to bean counters and the general public because "chauffeur" was the only word they heard. When appointed chief, I immediately reassigned those drivers, but it proved too late for budget reductions. I did receive permission from the city manager that began a process of creating the three division chief positions, one for each twenty-four-hour shift.

The primary role of a division chief was overseeing the ICS. Before recommending promotions of the three division chiefs, I met with all district chiefs and deputy chiefs of operations. After we went over the ICS program, I asked everyone for a secret vote naming three people, not including themselves, to fill those division chief positions. I wanted departmental confidence that those promoted represented the best emergency incident commanders.

Two of three district chiefs with the most votes had been fire chief candidates. The third was an interim fire chief before my promotion.

As I suspected, everyone voted for the same ones I would have chosen. One of those chosen was the hero lieutenant who, on his own, rose to the rank of district chief. We began implementing the ICS with only one shift. The other two shifts felt left out, and the old competition factor began taking hold. We finally allowed the other two shifts' participation and that softened resistance to change.

The original fire chief, Benjamin Franklin, sold fire marks that hung over the front doors of houses. The mark indicated that people had paid for fire protection, so when personnel arrived on the scene, if they saw the mark, volunteers attempted extinguishing the fire. If their mark wasn't visible, they all went away and let it burn. Fire prevention was on everyone's mind, maybe because fire insurance didn't exist back then.

As the fire service developed and before radios, commanding officers barked orders with megaphones. Those megaphones resembled large keyless bugles. Fire officers didn't have collar bars designating rank like the military. They had small bugles for rank designation. The lowest-ranking officer, usually a lieutenant, had one bugle, whereas captains had two parallel bugles. The next rank had two crossed bugles. The next had three, then four crossed, and finally, the fire chief had five crossed bugles. I don't have any two, three, or four cluster bugles in my collection.

An old saying about the onset of chaos was "When in doubt, run in circles, scream and shout." That response gave an impression of someone barking orders and controlling all functions. In fact, command broke down when it didn't occupy a fixed location, coordinate information, calmly give orders, and strategy was sacrificed for tactical management.

A manager in any organization who concentrates on all the activities of their subordinates, that is, micromanages, loses sight of the big picture. If someone micromanages in the private sector, organizations lose developmental growth. In public safety organizations, consequences are more life-threatening. If someone doesn't pay attention to overall strategy at an emergency, it could end in disaster.

The old tactics included simple sayings like "Put the wet stuff on the red stuff," or "Surround and drown." Those tactics evolved into a judicious use of water and consideration of ventilation, fire travel, rescue potential, air supply, utilities, safety, the position of all the fire companies, and many other critical components.

While implementing ICS, I reflected on the death of the Wichita fire chief and other fire personnel mentioned early on. If ICS had been in place at the time, those tragedies might not have occurred. During that Wichita operation, a lieutenant on top of an aerial ladder observed fire weakening a roof structure but had no idea firefighters were conducting operations inside. The ICS requirement for communication might have made a difference.

The proliferation of ICS in the fire service can be traced directly to Alan Brunacini, a fire chief from Phoenix, Arizona. He began with fire command, and that evolved into all incidents following a command structure. Fires, rescues, mass casualties, terrorist threats, and other incidents began using ICS when managing chaos. "Bruno" was a little shorter than average and slightly overweight, and sported a constant smile. He had closely cropped hair, wore large-rimmed glasses, and had a statuesque nose underlined by a Kilroy mustache. Bruno didn't invent ICS, but he sure preached the gospel more than anyone else. He prevented more firefighter injuries and deaths than any other individual I know. I've met a lot of people who could multitask, but Bruno could multithink and reason. Whatever the subject(s) open for discussion, his thoughts and advice always seemed worthwhile. His professional pride and humor made him a model fire chief.

In 1982, after we introduced ICS, we brought Bruno in for a seminar. His wit and charisma won over most remaining skeptics. Occasionally some hard-of-thinking firefighters could be heard saying, "You can't talk a fire out."

I always responded with "No, but you can get killed if you don't communicate."

21

FREE THOUGHTS, FREE SPEECH

Around 1980, the year of my appointment as fire chief, a secret national organization formed called the "Baggers." The primary revolutionaries included Bruno and Harry Diezel from Virginia Beach, Virginia. Others involved in that subversive group included Dick Moreno from Tucson and Pete Pederson from LA County, who later became a fire chief of Salt Lake City, Utah. They invited me into the group complete with a secret handshake. A lapel pin had the image of a paper bag with eyes, nose, and mouth cut out and the word *Bagger* beneath. That was an inner circle metaphor for our secret identities. I still have my pin. Some of my staff had a group picture taken with bags on their heads. That unauthorized protest happened because I refused to divulge any secrets of the Baggers.

The Baggers received the label "subversive" because they allowed free thought and encouraged free speech. That didn't seem right because free thought and speech could lead to innovation, an enemy of the status quo. The Baggers had two missions. First, we provided a freewheeling forum for discussion of issues the International Association of Fire Chiefs (IAFC) couldn't or wouldn't discuss. Second, we infiltrated the formal organization because rapid and true change could only come from inside an organization.

My task became difficult because I received an order to infiltrate the metropolitan fire chiefs' section of the IAFC. That group represented all member metropolises in the world with a population of more than two hundred thousand, or departments with four hundred total employees.

My predecessor in Wichita told me the metro chiefs would be my best contacts for networking. Dodd Miller from Dallas and Herman Brice from Miami had already moved up in the organization and became good mentors. I eventually became president of the organization.

The Baggers, which was a networking group, met east of the Mississippi, and Harry tried moderating. The next time we met west of the Mississippi, and Bruno helped Harry try moderating. We started meetings by discussing significant programs that worked well for each department. We then talked about programs that hadn't worked well. Finally, we discussed upcoming initiatives that individuals were considering. Brutality defined our questioning, but those sessions didn't let us hide flaws in our reasoning. We defended or changed our approach to the issues we faced. That group finally started allowing others into the circle (some didn't even have five bugles), and that signaled the beginning of the slow demise of the organization. By the time group participation slowed, some participants thought the Baggers were a group that got together with a sack lunch. I've heard rumors they have reconstituted, albeit without the sick humor. The modern IAFC now offers educational programs and services for all members. The 2019–20 IAFC president, Gary Ludwig, fire chief of Champaign, Illinois, is a nationally recognized authority on EMS and an accomplished author.

The Wichita Fire Department participated in another organization, the National Fire Academy (NFA). During the 1980s, firefighters attended the NFA with little monetary commitment from local communities. We sent so many people that an NFA administrator told me we had more attendees in one year than any other department in the country. That participation allowed interaction among fire service personnel from across the country. Homeschooling for organizations didn't always provide the best opportunity for organizational growth and development.

We also sent people who helped develop NFA courses. I helped develop manuals on pumper and ladder company operations. John Bode, who took Jim Cloud's place as executive officer, also helped develop a course called Micro Computers in the Fire Service.

We considered installing a new radio system and connecting each station with computers for report writing and communicating. That doesn't sound like much now, but in 1983 mainframes still ruled. John Bode, stationed in operations, had applied for the executive officer position. We asked each candidate two main questions. The first:

"What experience do you have with radio systems?"

"On my days off I service the downlink for the Boeing Company," John replied.

The second: "What experience do you have with computers?"

"I have written over one million lines of computer code."

John ended up designing and installing PCs and connecting all our facilities, but he provided other innovations. Previous computer modeling for locating fire station sites all used mainframe computers and took months to complete. John came up with a program called Fire Station Location and Mapping Environment (FLAME). He went to a library and downloaded any county street files on his laptop, folded in his software, and sent any community a disc.

Communities then computer-modeled potential fire station locations and displayed a local road network in colors representing minutes of travel time from any given location. For three minutes' travel time, all roads surrounding a proposed location were in one color, and the colors changed to signal four minutes, five minutes, and so on. Some politicians preferred familiar maps with pretty colors to abstract concepts. John, an innovative leader for the WFD, developed computer-generated church bell chimes and clocks so accurate that military installations around the world used them. One of his company clocks (made by BRG Precision Products) used to sit in the Oval Office.

My favorite memory of John's cognitive ability occurred when he smashed out a second-story window frame at the Bethel Baptist Church fire with the end of an aerial ladder. His quick thinking provided fresh air and an escape route for an interior-attack firefighting company that was disoriented and had empty air tanks. I can say that hidden talent, similar to John Bode's, permeated the fire service. Firefighters in every fire organization I worked with helped solve problems of a normal business nature or at an emergency scene.

The WFD also got involved in better methods for rescue, including the trench, high angle, and water rescue. In each of those endeavors, some member or members of the department had a special interest, and we let them run with it. Firefighters considered providing the best level of service and increasing the chances of successful rescue attempts. I wanted their safety considered in every operation.

Leadership didn't mean hollering, "Charge!" Leadership meant telling people what we wanted and why, then staying out of the way while they planned the route. Besides providing support, a key element in leadership included taking the blame if something went wrong or someone, like a politician, became upset. Naturally, problems arose along the way, but I didn't fall into the trap of telling subordinates my answers.

I used to say, "Don't bring me problems; bring me solutions, and I will help you pick the best one."

My help always took the form of questions and other considerations. Developing subordinates who knew *what* to think seemed easy. Developing subordinates who knew *how* to think required more effort but yielded better long-term results.

I had no problem in making a decision that needed more immediate attention, in administration or operations. If an administrative subordinate needed an immediate answer, I provided one, given the information available.

A quick operational decision came at one fire I still have a picture of today, the old Salvation Army building in downtown Wichita. The building consisted of heavy timber construction with a brick exterior and wood floors oil-soaked from a leaky forklift. The initial cause of fire was vagrants trying to stay warm in an abandoned building. Whatever the cause, the building became a containment operation when fire companies first arrived.

The notification of additional companies meant the dispatcher also notified me. When I arrived, the roof had burned off and the fire was so hot that two small thermal tornadoes danced in the fiery furnace. The building sat on a corner lot, with a vacant lot on one side, so no exposure problems existed on three sides. Across an alley sat an older building. An aerial platform was set in the vacant lot and pushed the flames toward that building, causing cracked windows and smoke inside. The incident commander redirected water, barely preventing the second structure from catching fire.

The actual scare came after the fire, when an officer deployed fire hose lines for hot-spot extinguishment. I noticed an upper brick corner separating from one side of the building because of the heating and cooling effect. I strolled over to an officer in charge of that operation, mentioned the potential issue, and stepped back. My gaze shifted from the separating brick to the firefighter with a hose line to an officer who had engaged in a casual conversation with others. No doubt their discussion focused on a foundation they had saved. Never mind someone forgot a basic consideration of protecting exposures first, like the only nearby building, and attacking the fire later.

The firefighter with the hose line couldn't see the corner separating because he had a view from one side. As the wall started falling, I screamed at the firefighter. "Drop your hose line and get back!" He readily complied, and a brick wall fell on his hose line. I immediately felt the anger building deep inside but resisted the temptation to make that officer brand-new (I'll explain that term in the next chapter). The firefighter's name was Pink. Another observer, LJ, laughed and told Pink, with hyperbole, that I had saved his life. That broke my angry trance, as I began thinking about my dislike when superior officers reprimanded someone in front of others. I walked away and thought about the events overnight.

That's one of only two times I ever intervened in any operation, but I never took command away from any officer because of what the hero lieutenant had taught me. The next day, I visited with the on-duty division chief, Jerry Laughary, who smiled and calmly said in that slow, familiar drawl, "It looks like you had a little exposure problem last night." I knew he would calmly critique the overnight events.

He had no idea how much I wished he had been the incident commander. Other chiefs recommended the hero lieutenant for promotion through the ranks to district chief. I recommended him for promotion to division chief partly because he had a doctorate in common sense. Also, his peer chiefs had selected him as one of the top three chief officers for promotion to division chief. He also stood chairs up with the flex of a wrist. I agreed with Deputy Floyd that the feat resulted from willpower, but I also noticed how individuals who accomplished that feat all had strong hands and disproportionately huge wrists.

22

MAKING PEOPLE BRAND-NEW

One of our fire prevention programs focused on high-risk properties that offered places of unique firefighting challenges, like high-rise buildings. The building department, with the fire department's support, passed codes that retroactively required sprinkler system installation in high-rise buildings. Many cities did that in response to the MGM Grand hotel fire in 1980 that killed eighty-five people and injured scores of civilians and firefighters. There's always an outcry after tragedies, but it doesn't last long. Many older high-rise buildings didn't have sprinkler systems. Instead, those buildings had fire detection systems and dry standpipes for firefighting. Standpipes were large-diameter steel pipes that ran up through enclosed stairwells with hose connections at ground level, and on each floor. Ground-level connections provided water to the pipes, and each floor had hose connections for fighting fire on any floor.

The detection systems detected smoke and, in some cases, heat. It made no sense to me that someone would spend money on detecting fire but do nothing to extinguish a fire at its origin, as a well-maintained sprinkler system would. Stopping fire at its origin causes less damage, less business interruptions, and cheaper insurance rates, and doesn't put firefighters in harm's way.

We couldn't realistically shut down those buildings lacking sprinklers, so we began bringing buildings that remodeled into compliance. We made the other building owners aware of the new codes and began an educational program. We pointed out that owners' fire insurance costs would be lower, and if amortized over time, much of the sprinkler construction costs could be recouped. We suggested that if owners planned on flipping a building, a sprinkler system added more value, made the property more marketable, and produced a good return on investment. The issue of liability inevitably found its way into any conversation about sprinkler protection.

VIPs, in particular, demanded buildings with sprinkler systems. We mentioned that First Lady Rosalynn Carter, who visited Wichita, was awakened by a false alarm. Although nothing happened, she praised the building owner's safety efforts.

Although we proceeded slowly and granted time for compliance, some owners began making excuses. Some said their insurance companies told them premiums would be higher because of potential water damage. I enjoyed that last excuse. We told them we couldn't recommend a particular insurance company but suggested they rebid their insurance needs. It was interesting watching fire insurance quotes come down and potential water damage issues disappear.

In this area, the department was too complacent in code enforcement. For example, five years earlier a bureaucrat omitted a sprinkler system in a new high-rise city hall building because of construction cost overruns. After becoming fire chief, I had funding included in the capital improvement program for retrofitting a sprinkler system in city hall. The fire marshal at the time, Jim Cloud, and the plans examination specialist, Bob Camfield, managed our retroactive sprinkler program.

Number five on the previously mentioned long list of changes included our continued arson investigation commitment. The arson task force consisted of fire investigators, police, and a prosecutor from the district attorney's office. As usual, grant money ran out, and we made decisions on continuing the program.

I viewed arsonists the same way police chiefs viewed criminals who shot at officers, because arsonists can kill firefighters.

The fire department succeeded in having state legislation passed that gave our investigators full police powers. The district attorney's office continued working with us, although they couldn't dedicate a full-time person exclusively for arson prosecution. Assistant DA David Moses proved invaluable because he led us out of the wilderness of prosecuting arson, one of the most difficult crimes to prove. He educated our investigators on what he needed for prosecuting a case requiring motive, method, and intent. David always dressed as if he owned a clothing store. His impeccable appearance matched his nitpicky requests for more and complete information, which made investigators better at investigating and detailing follow-up. An arson conviction helped put local gangster George Poulos in prison.

Whenever our investigators received a potential arson fire tip, they acted proactively. Investigators immediately met with property owners and shared our information for the good of their business. That approach worked because we never had a fire in any of those businesses. By continuing the arson task force program, we had a high arrest and conviction rate.

Bob Camfield also examined plans for new or remodeled construction projects. The fire department previously didn't review plans for construction projects at WSU because of state law and it being state property, which exempted it from local jurisdictions. That happened in the mid-1960s with the change to state control from the former Wichita University. We knew that because of Important Person, whom we encountered with Captain Tom Massey.

Wichita State's basketball teams varied between good and great. During my tenure as fire chief, the team did particularly well and even beat KU in the NCAA regional in 1981. As a result, they needed additional seating in their home venue. The athletic department wanted more seating over the arena's entrances and exits. We looked for safe ways of complying with the building owner's wishes. Instead of rejecting increased occupancy limits, we suggested owners consider all construction options for more exits, figure the costs, and decide if the increased capacity justified additional costs. That left decision-makers with a business decision.

Concerning WSU, we suggested the athletic department pay off-duty fire prevention personnel for keeping aisles open and providing emergency crowd control, and submit plans for our examination. I thought we agreed on plans examination, but Important Person balked at submitting plans to the WFD. I suggested Important Person contact the Board of Regents for a budget request to start a university fire department.

When asked why, I explained, "We don't want our firefighters subjected to the dangers of fighting fire in a building that doesn't comply with our latest fire codes. Also, the latest codes provide more safety for all occupants." We ultimately agreed that pending new state codes replicated ours; that gave Important Person an out. From that point on, the department reviewed all plans, and I received two complimentary tickets to all WSU basketball games, which I gave to fire prevention personnel. It made no sense to me that some state colleges and universities opted out of modern code compliance in favor of older state codes in order to save on construction costs. Tragedy had struck before in campus housing and other buildings across the country. But still, they insisted on maintaining their independence from local jurisdictions.

Wichita State University made me a better and more successful individual, and I believe we contributed to a safer environment for all faculty, staff, students, and visitors. In 2014, while attending a granddaughter's graduation ceremony, I noticed the beautiful and code-compliant arena renovation.

Near my administrative end, a "tiny profit margin" owner attempted sidetracking our high-rise retrofitting efforts with his political connection. His requested meeting with me didn't start well because it began with a threat. By then I could control the visceral part of my reaction to being threatened or challenged in any way. The incident that turned me around occurred on campus. I got into a fight with a guy over a parking space. I won the fight, but later wondered about losing my self-control over such a trivial issue.

That's the last time I ever resorted to physical violence, ending a process that began in high school. Maybe a seed was planted at age five when I received an inflatable Joe Palooka punching doll that popped up every time I knocked it over. Maybe it began with stories about one of my uncles. Maybe it started with being told, "Stand up for yourself, and if someone threatens you, punch him in the nose," like Pee Wee did. In high school, there were two unwritten rules: no weapons and no fighting on school grounds while school is in session.

Fighting also had a way of quieting bigoted behavior. One of my best friends in high school and afterward, Jerry Witt, used that approach. Jerry and his twin brother, Terry, wrestled and fought. The alpha male of our group, Terry, fought at the drop of a hat. Jerry required provoking.

I knew about Jerry being gay because of a long discussion we had before he traveled to the Ozarks for work at a resort in the summer of 1963. The three-hour discussion covered many areas, all helping reeducate a wide-eyed high school junior. The biggest relief came when I brought up the subject of a predatory pedophile teacher who taught at a junior high school, and who made advances toward me.

I told Jerry about the teacher's offer to take me to a basketball game at North High School. Since I would soon attend North,

I readily accepted his offer. I didn't think much about it until the teacher pulled into our driveway. He remained in the car, and Mom wondered out loud why he didn't come to our door. I was puzzled when we entered the gym, and a couple of junior high classmates leaned against a wall. One of the boys whispered to the other, pointed at us, and grinned.

After the game, the teacher said he needed to stop by his apartment for a minute. "Come on in, and I'll show you my apartment." We went inside, and he immediately began showing me some pornographic magazines. The teacher kept getting closer to me, all the time pointing at the pictures. When he put his hand on my shoulder, he was close enough that I smelled his stale cigarette breath.

I tossed the magazine on the counter. "I need to go home now."

My heart pounded so hard I knew he could hear it, but I didn't want to show fear. The teacher asked, "Don't you like the pictures?"

"They're okay, but I want to go home *now*!" I headed for the back door.

All the way home the teacher kept saying that I shouldn't tell anybody about the pictures because we could both get into trouble. For a long time after that, I felt guilty for being so stupid. I told the story to the classmate I saw in the gymnasium, and he said he thought everyone knew about the teacher. That teacher was the only model I had for a gay man until my discussion with Jerry.

Jerry listened to my story, laughed at first when I asked him about the pedophile being gay, then turned to me. "No, those people have a special place in hell reserved for them."

"You do know some people say the same thing about you."

Jerry lowered his head and with wet eyes quietly said, "Oh, I know."

Jerry said that his "condition" wasn't treatable nor did he want it treated even if that was possible. One thing stumped both of us. Some high school boys referred to Thursdays as "queer day," when discussing one's clothing or effeminate behavior. We each thought, wrongly, that our unique perspectives might lead to that observation's origin. A standard clothing ensemble included a white T-shirt, blue jeans, white gym socks, and black loafers.

If fashion bigots saw a pastel color, print, or weird matching clothes, the ritual comment was "Hey, this isn't Thursday." Not long after our discussion that night, I started wearing my favorite color of purple (lavender) and my new second favorite color—pink.

Jerry dispelled many other long-held beliefs that evening, but I remember one comment more than others: "Queers aren't in competition with you."

For years after that, when someone asked my opinion on gay people, I said, "Gay men are no competition in my marketplace. I'm not a preacher, so morality is a sermon left for other people." Jerry helped change the way I viewed people and I gave him the only things he requested—understanding and friendship.

Jerry finally came out in the fall of 1963, and I was present for his unorthodox announcement. Coming out in the 1960s didn't include the same celebrations, acceptance, and rights people see today.

Jerry and I didn't look for fighting opportunities, but we didn't look away, either. On one occasion we stood across the street from North High, having just finished our evening meal of a burger, fries, and a Coke. While visiting with a classmate, I didn't see or hear what some guy said as his car idled through the parking lot, but Jerry did. Before I could turn around, Jerry walked to the car and said something to the driver. The guy got out of his car, and they both walked over to the school lawn.

Jerry tripped the guy, jumped on top of him, and finished a quick pounding by the time I had crossed the street. I watched as Jerry got to his feet and asked, "How does it feel to have your butt kicked by a queer?"

We left, laughing, but the message went out from kids who gathered and watched the fight. I asked Jerry why he did that, and he said he got the idea from me. He recalled the time I put a thumping on Mike Flowers. That encounter began while I minded my own business. During a lunch break, I sat on the hallway floor and leaned against the wall outside of my next class, reading my English lit book. Mike and two of his friends came strolling down the hall from my left. I casually glanced up from my reading and followed them with my eyes as they passed in front of me.

Mike glanced back at me, stopped, and asked, "What are you looking at?"

My usual response to that question had been "Nothing." That gave an interrogator an out, and me the satisfaction of knowing what I meant. But something about the three of them made me respond, "Not much."

Mike took two more steps, turned back around, and let the bird fly. I got up, walked straight to him, and asked, "Do you know where the Minisa building across the river is?"

"Yes."

I looked into his eyes and offered, "I'll meet you behind that building after school, and we'll settle this."

I didn't know if Mike would bring his reinforcements or not, so I brought Jerry and Terry as my seconds. I knew Jerry and Terry would hold the others off, so I could deal with them one at a time. I lunged at Mike, tripped him with my left leg behind his right, and jumped on top of him.

After a few well-placed blows, I asked, "Had enough?"

"No," he shot back.

After that, Mike received another punch every time he answered no to my question, "Do you give?" Finally, in frustration and with no desire to inflict more facial damage, I said, "Okay, you win," and walked away without a scratch. Mike's two friends left before the fight ended.

Not long after Jerry's abrupt coming out that night on the school lawn, one of my classmates made a homophobic comment to me about his sexuality.

"I'll relay your thoughts to Jerry."

"Oh no, no, I was just kidding."

He knew Jerry could clean his clock as well. For me, Jerry put a human face on a denigrated class of people.

Even though I hadn't been in a fight in years, that parking space tussle brought back cool days of old when I felt threatened or challenged. From that point on, instead of fighting, I made people "brand-new" with my mouth, sometimes with the use of bad language. Making someone brand-new meant you changed their behavior or caused them to rethink their actions. A verbal punch could be longer-lasting, and vastly more stunning, particularly if conveying the stinging truth. More important, resorting to physical violence meant that someone got to you, and I didn't want to show that. Over time I lessened my use of foul language in confrontational situations.

My grandmother and mother had rules on bad language reinforced by a bar of soap in the mouth. Because of language barriers, my parents didn't discuss certain topics. I could've used a good open discussion on sex and strangers (sexual predators) before I turned fifteen. Included in that discussion should've been a brief revisit of the ingrained notion that we should always respect and obey our elders. Too many communication barriers existed without building artificial ones. Open communication in a family should've been where we discussed "how to think" decisions. That's why I insisted on my children expressing themselves any way they chose.

Even though I didn't have that pedophile as one of my teachers, he still carried the title of teacher. That meant I felt particularly honored when he asked about taking me to a game and didn't question anything until those final moments in his house. After reflecting on my bad experience, I realized that's where I developed my lack of fear of people, particularly those in a position of authority. Respect remained, but blind obedience—no.

§

All my former visceral reactions from violence to swearing melted away as I sat across the desk, listening to the words that just came out of Tiny Profit Margin's mouth. "I just came from Politician, and he suggested I remind you that inspectors can be removed from the annual budget. Politician also told me that the city council could amend fire codes to grandfather in buildings like mine." We attended high school together, so maybe he remembered my reputation for getting into fights and tried provoking me into doing or saying something unprofessional. Here I sat in a threatening situation, but I realized my response needed to make him brand-new and go directly to Politician.

"I will openly oppose any attempt to weaken the fire code, and I will use your building as an example. If I lose one inspector, I will retrain over three hundred firefighters and go through this town like crap through a goose." I then added, "Don't you ever threaten me again." I meant both of those comments for Politician, as I meant my statement to the media after a practical high-rise training exercise. "If one-quarter of any unsprinklered high-rise floor is involved in fire, our ability to quickly deploy enough personnel to stop it is questionable."

That quote, along with the Tiny Profit Margin encounter comments, was more than Politician could stand. He walked over to both deputy chiefs and me while we sat having lunch in the city hall cafeteria. "I don't appreciate what you said in the paper."

I thought about telling him that taking advantage of technologies, like sprinkler systems, answered some concerns regarding personnel reductions. His bullying tactics and subversion of the manager/council form of government that prohibited political interference changed my mind. I looked straight into his eyes and continued smiling. "What I said about personnel reductions and unsprinklered high-rise buildings took any liability for some future preventable catastrophe off me and placed it right on you." With a disgusted look on his face, he turned and walked away.

That comment sank in and must've gotten around because the mayor had only one comment regarding my newspaper statement: "I guess the best defense (regarding personnel reductions) is a good offense." Nobody attempted a code change grandfathering in older, remodeled high-rise buildings from retroactive sprinkler requirements during my remaining tenure.

23

SUBSTANCE VS. APPEARANCE

My fire chief appointment brought a change from my working twenty-four-hour shifts to an eight-hour day shift. That let my son, Derek, the pride of my second failed marriage, move in with me, and I received residential custody. I enjoyed bonding with him and having someone to both confide in and advise. Derek attended my old high school. A fellow student of his was Barry Sanders, who became an NFL Hall of Famer. Barry was a first-class gentleman and good role model for any athlete; he overshadowed all other athletes. His celebration and reason why, after every touchdown, will never be bested. He merely handed the ball to the referee and rejoined his team that helped get him to the end zone. He displayed his conquering greatness with dignity.

Derek had no difficulty in surpassing my academic achievements. Derek's gentle and loving nature made it easy for me as a parent. If he saw injustice or felt someone treated him unfairly, he spoke up, but unlike me, Derek spoke up with low-level intensity. Derek rarely needed discipline.

I sometimes think about the time lost with my two children. I can't recapture those times, but all their lives I've reassured them in every birthday card, Christmas card, phone conversation, and visit with a simple ending phrase: "I love you." My daughter, Shelley, like my son, didn't need discipline, either; although one time I administered some corporal punishment to both of them.

Because I spent too much time on my education and career, I tried sharing more time with my two children on vacations and weekends.

Sometimes we went to Colorado in the summer; other times we vacationed in winter to ski. On one vacation we traveled from Wichita to California to visit my relocated mother and siblings. Shelley was about nine years old, and Derek about five. I purchased a truck with a camper for our cross-country journey. Summertime in Arizona was brutal. The two miscreants played on an overhead bed that extended over the cab. I had my cab air conditioner set on frantic, and things seemed tolerable. I had removed the back window of the truck cab, and a rubber boot sealed the space between the camper and truck. That provided direct access into the camper and tolerable airflow, or so I thought.

In the overhead camper playpen, a window cranked out for ventilation when we parked. I provided specific instructions about what would happen if they opened the window during full travel speed. I know they both understood because they nodded their heads up and down. The sound of glass shattering above my head made me pull over and enter the enclosed dungeon of discipline. To be sure, we went over the previous tutorial on that specific window and the same nodding of both heads occurred again. I didn't allow any sidetracking by asking the question of who opened the window because the time had arrived for negative reinforcement. Both of them lay on their stomachs, and with as little force as I could muster, they received one swat with the palm of my hand similar to the one I received for my sacrilegious act those many years ago.

As I climbed back into the truck and made my way to the nearest stop for repairs, I heard both of them giggling. The humiliation intensified as whispers and giggles alternated for several miles. Revenge became mine, though, when we stopped at one of those roadside curio shops. The shop had a small donkey that held still for pictures. After many direct orders, they stood close to the donkey. Before the shutter snapped, the little donkey opened his mouth and made that braying noise only a donkey can make. After development, the picture showed two bolting miscreants captured midstride. I still look at that picture and laugh, but they don't see the humor. However, they do laugh at the story of my feeble attempt at discipline.

My son got caught at everything I got away with at his age. I balked at intervening on his behalf when something went wrong. I thought if I tried making my children's lives easier that potentially took away the lessons learned from misfortunes or mistakes. Although I didn't have much extra money, it seemed that handing them money without an appreciation for what it took to make that money might make them lose their incentive for success. To me, unearned money gave children an appearance of success but risked the removal of a substantive building block (work ethic) of character, because that's the way my parents raised me.

How I saw my fatherly role made me reflect on my own father's life. I was thirteen years old when my father died from lung cancer six months after his diagnosis. Back in 1960 doctors opened a patient from midchest, under the arm, then around to midback. Doctors then went in and cut out the cancer, closed the wound, and administered radiation. When my father came home from the hospital and recuperated, he needed care, which my mother provided. It appeared that he was healing, and our idyllic life would continue, but then Dad's condition worsened.

One day when I came home from neighborhood playing, Mom said, "Your dad is in the bathtub, and you should go help bathe him because he is too weak to bathe himself." I walked into the bathroom, leaned over the tub, and first noticed Dad's red eyes, a result of crying. He lost a lot of weight and had no hair because of radiation treatments. I remembered several male church members who buzz-cut their hair in support of Dad. A mostly bald Captain Kendal Seaman was one of them.

Because of his weakened condition, we stopped several times and let him rest. When I finished drying Dad, dressing him, and helping him into bed, he apologized to me. I kissed him and told him, "That's okay." I thought at the time he, a proud man, was apologizing for me seeing his nakedness and helplessness. Later I realized he was apologizing for his certain death and leaving me without a father. Even with all the pain, suffering, and humiliation he went through, he was focused on love, care, and concern for me, my sister, and Mom. He'd felt like he let his family down.

About a week later Mom opened the back door and called me in from playing. She said my neighborhood friend Toni Blake wanted me to visit at her home. At Toni's home, we barely struck up a conversation when an ambulance slowly drove past. Shortly after that, Mom called and had Mrs. Blake tell me to come back home.

When I walked in the front door, Mom said, "Have a seat on the sofa next to me. That ambulance just took Dad back to the veteran's hospital, and I didn't want you to see that."

"When will he come back?"

"I'm not sure. Dad needs some medical attention. I've arranged for your vacation with Dad's sister, Aunt Blanche, and Uncle Clarence. They will be here this evening. What you need to do is pray for Dad's recovery."

I remember riding in the back of their old Chevy until I fell asleep on the journey to Carthage, Missouri. I realized later Mom had all she could handle with taking care of my sister and Dad's imminent death. I was too naive and immature to provide any comfort.

My aunt and uncle ran a small neighborhood grocery store with living quarters in the back. I remembered images of that store when reading *I Know Why the Caged Bird Sings*. We'd just finished dinner one evening when the phone rang. By now I realized my praying probably wasn't working. My aunt's responses on the phone were quiet, and when she turned to me, I asked, "Is Dad gone?"

With tears in her eyes, she answered, "Yes."

I waited until bedtime before crying because I remembered Dad telling me that now I needed to be a man. The reality of that statement suddenly set in.

I don't remember the trip back to Wichita, or much of anything else until Dad's funeral at the Olivet Baptist Church, at 3440 West Thirteenth Street. I remember passing his coffin and saying, "Goodbye, Dad," because he told me that's what he said when his father died, only he called his father "Pop." We buried Dad in the northwest corner of the cemetery at Hillside and Twenty-First Street. We came full circle because the first place we rented was on Jardine Drive, a few blocks away. I had no idea that would be the future area of my higher education and service area for Fire Station 10.

I always remembered the church's address because, as a firefighter, we memorized which side of the street carried even- or odd-numbered addresses. Our home address, 222 South Tracy, became my memory technique for north and south streets. That was our first owned home. Mom was a nomadic type, so we lived in three rental properties before the house on Tracy. I attended three different junior high schools.

Respect for my father only grew after he died. I sat on the sofa reading some papers Mom produced for legal reasons and noticed the date on their marriage license. Although slow at math, I knew the human gestation period exceeded those few short months before my birth date. Without beating around the bush, as the old country saying goes, I asked, "What's this?"

Mom stood on the floor furnace with a sheepish expression. "I got pregnant before your dad and I got married. Are you ashamed of me?"

"Of course not. I'm happy to be alive."

Years later I played golf at Sim Park golf course, before the new course design. I finished playing the No. 2 hole and walked across the street toward the tee box for No. 3. A couple of young women milled around outside of the two-story redbrick building. I asked my playing partner, "What's that building?"

"That's a home for unwed mothers."

I recalled Mom telling me that, besides being blamed for getting pregnant, unwed mothers were sometimes sent by their families to relatives' homes until after giving birth. Sometimes they kept their babies, and sometimes the mothers put them up for adoption before returning home. That way families avoided shame, and community life went on. I thought, *But not for the mother and child. Their lives never just—went on.*

Many years later Mom and I discussed the adoption of my younger sister. Mom paused for a long time, then told me the rest of the story that she had left out during our conversation years before. My father was incapable of having children. She then identified my biological father: Bobby Sailes from Oklahoma. Bobby courted my mother until she became pregnant, then informed her he already had a family and would soon depart. My daughter once asked if I harbored any ill will toward Bobby or my mother. I replied that I didn't, but like her, I would've liked to have known that biological side of my medical history. No matter what has happened, I've never seen myself as a victim. When something went wrong, as mentioned earlier, call it *tuition*, learn something, and move on. I learned about speaking openly to my children on any subject and always expressed my love for them.

The man who raised me as his son kept me from being a bastard, although some have since proclaimed otherwise. I imagined his life for all those years, knowing I wasn't biologically his son but still giving me his love and concern. Dad also gave me his name, and that's why I've been so proud of my name. But Dad's concern for me was founded on his love for my mother, which formed when he first saw her. Until Dad's death, marriage and a happy family life seemed uncomplicated and easy.

After my father died, Mom needed work, so she enrolled in beauty school. The study material was particularly hard for her because of her poor education. She stayed up late at night studying while raising two children and dealing with grief. I never heard one complaint. At age thirteen, I learned the values of perseverance and hard work. My parents told me I could be anything I wanted to be or do anything I wanted to do, and they made me believe it.

My father was a newspaper pressman for the *Wichita Beacon*. Dad died not long before the newspaper merged with the *Wichita Eagle*, becoming the *Eagle/Beacon*, and later the *Wichita Eagle*. Dad worked in a loud environment on a dirty job. The one time I remember visiting his workplace, he wore blue-jean overalls. Black ink covered his overalls and hands. I never saw his hands like that and reflected on holding his hand in church. His fingernails always appeared perfectly manicured and clean.

I watched the giant rolls of white paper as they moved around on small four-wheel dollies that traveled on small train tracks. After the pressman inserted a new roll, the presses began creeping slowly. Gradually the speed of wide paper rolls picked up, and clack, clack, clacking sounds grew deafeningly loud.

I still remember Dad's pride when they ran a color picture in the Sunday edition. I also remember one fall Sunday morning as he sat at the dining table in his red and green flannel shirt and slacks. I walked in from finishing my early morning paper route. Dad asked, "Did you see the front-page picture?"

"Yes, but I didn't pay any attention to it."

"The colors didn't align and left a blurred image." At age twelve, my only thoughts centered on finishing my route, hustling home to breakfast, and getting ready for church. I suspect Dad's quiet criticism focused on why a pressman didn't catch the mistake before copies hit the street.

Mom said she wished he had lived to see the newspapers merge. Years later I found out that Dad was a union negotiator for the pressmen. One time some difficulties arose in reaching an agreement over some issue. Dad simply closed his book and proclaimed that management could let him know when they were serious. People have asked the old question, "Is it nature or nurture?" I always said yes.

About one year after Dad died, Mom remarried. Our stepfather brought three daughters to the marriage, and they had two daughters and a son. He needed a mother for his children, and Mom had an opportunity for the large family she always wanted. My younger sister, Jeanie, became part of that now-sizable family. Jeanie never got over our father's death because he completely doted on her. When Mom remarried, Jeanie was thrust into an environment of competition for affection from a stepfather who didn't express his love the same way as Dad. The stepfather's religious fanaticism and poor parental skills devastated Jeanie. She married at a young age and got away from that environment.

I was part of the family for three years but always on the go. Home for me was a place to sleep, grab an occasional meal, and then head out to high school or a job. I didn't get to know my two half sisters, Lisa and Karla, or my half brother, Brent, until later in life. I was married within a year after high school, and the entire family moved to California shortly thereafter. My stepfather joined his religious congregation's home base, and Mom eagerly anticipated challenges in a new environment.

My mother helped raise all those children and me. She loved and adored each of us. Her capacity for loving and caring about others seemed unlimited. Before the remarriage, I had a high school friend who needed a place to stay before shipping out as a merchant seaman.

Mom never questioned the situation. As she did for all people, she saw the substance in my friend Doug "Whitey" Anderson. He picked up the nickname Whitey in high school because of his platinum-blond hair. He was the sergeant at arms for our high school graduating class. Mom insisted that Doug come and live with us because her helping desire knew no bounds. Doug later became a Navy SEAL, and now he resides in Colorado. We remain good friends.

That's the way my mother lived her life, and from her came my desire to help people without regard to their status in life. She ingrained substance over appearance in me from the beginning. I learned the more I concentrated on someone's appearance, the further I moved from their recognizable substance. People who have character and substance appreciate their blessings. More importantly, I've learned they don't complain about adversity; rather they adapt, improvise, grow, and move on.

24

IMPROVISE, ADAPT

Wichita, the largest city in Kansas and known as the air capital of the world, has been the home to Beech, Cessna, Learjet, and Boeing. At one time Wichita companies built over half of all aircraft in the world. With McConnell Air Force Base, the main commercial airport, the Boeing facility, and outlying airstrips, crashes seemed inevitable.

The most tragic crash involved an air refueling tanker that went down in northeast Wichita in 1965. That disaster occurred a few blocks from Fire Station 10. Anecdotal information said the station firefighters didn't need an alarm because they felt the vibration of the crash and saw the horrific fireball. When the fire truck pulled out of the station, the captain got on the radio. "Make this a general alarm and send me everything you have."

When asked what assignment, he reportedly said, "Pick any house on fire."

During my tenure as fire chief, one plane crashed at Mid-Continent, now called Dwight D. Eisenhower National Airport. While driving west on US 54, I heard the call over my car radio. Without information, the mind made things up. I pictured the previously described tragedy and responded by following a fire truck past where my flying career ended and on to the crash site. The jet crashed short of the runway, and an airport crew had extinguished the small fire.

I inquired about the pilots and any passengers when one of our investigators told me what had happened. An aircraft mechanic who could start and taxi a jet reportedly got hopped up on drugs and decided that was the time for his solo flight. At least I studied and took lessons. He took off, became airborne, and barely missed the control tower. He flew around one time with wings alternating up and down. As he approached the landing, he flew too low and slow and bellied in short of the runway. When he climbed out of the plane, police arrested him. He mumbled that he wanted another plane so he could take his girlfriend up.

The senior executive on scene lamented that they had already sold the plane. He didn't see the humor when someone said something about a new marketing strategy: "See, even our untrained mechanics can fly our planes."

I also remember a Learjet that crashed shortly after takeoff from Mid-Continent Airport when I was a teenager. The plane clipped the hedgerow treetops and landed in my boss's wheat field. The farmer I worked for had me get in the truck, and we left the farmyard.

When we arrived on the scene, a plane lay in the middle of the field, but it hadn't burned, probably because the jet engines had flamed out. A nearby farmer took his tractor and plowed a circle around the plane to keep any potential fire from spreading. He reported that the pilot and FAA certifying official jumped out of the plane and ran before it slid to a complete stop. The adaptive quick actions of the nearby farmer fascinated me.

The farmer I worked for displayed quick thinking and deliberate actions as well. I had purchased my first vehicle, a 1962 VW beetle. When I drove into the farmyard, the farmer came over and checked out my VW. His curiosity focused on the jack because it traveled on a steel rod. The farmer watched as I demonstrated how it worked. He said nothing else, but one day we climbed in his truck and drove to a pasture where one of his young cows was having difficulty giving birth.

When we arrived, birthing had started but stopped with part of the calf hanging outside of the birthing canal. The farmer took out a long steel rod with a curved plate on one end and a VW jack next to the plate. He placed the curved plate against the cow's butt, tied a strap to the calf, and jacked the calf out. Maybe that's when I began looking at what situations can be instead of what they are, and further learned the need for improvising. Use of that skill would become valuable in situations I faced as a firefighter and fire chief.

I also remember when the farmer gave me a ten-cent-per-hour

raise above the minimum wage. Plowing fields at night for extra money helped, but after about a month another farmhand (paid less per hour than me) received more working hours than me. I knew we neared the plowing season's end and wanted as many hours as possible. The farmer had rewarded me with a raise because of my work ethic. So I adapted and asked the farmer, "If you drop the ten-cents-per-hour raise will more hours come my way?"

The farmer smiled. "Yes."

I soon worked more hours. Life is interesting—all you have to do is pay attention.

In the summer of 1985, at age thirty-eight, I completed my eighteenth year of fire department service and fifth year as fire chief. My sixteen-year-old son and I finished playing golf in the morning and sat on our front porch, staring at our vegetable garden as the smell of tomato plants still lingered on my fingers. My thoughts focused on personal goals. Accomplishing set goals defined both my professional and personal life. I had a small wish list and checked off most of that list. I had already ridden a bull and a bronco and did well on the horse until it ran to one end of the corral, then made an immediate ninety-degree right turn. The bull wasn't much of a bull, but as I always said when asked, "It was probably like eating a skunk; I got all I wanted real quick."

I had accomplished one of two remaining adventures, skydiving, five years earlier. Flying in a military jet remained my only unfulfilled adventure. The opportunity came while participating in a community outreach program with McConnell AFB. Once a month local dignitaries played the nine-hole golf course on base. I knew for years that the military let dignitaries and politicians fly in their jets. While paired with the base commander one day, I asked about flying in one of their jets. The colonel said sure, but it seemed like a lengthy wait.

Four weeks previously the newspaper had run a story about a newly elected sheriff who flew in one of the jets. The next opportunity came soon, and I thanked the commander for our mutual aid agreement, which benefited both fire departments. The commander knew about providing their aircraft firefighting vehicle if needed because he had to approve it before a response from the base. Our department provided base firefighters with structural firefighting training and potential backup. I said, "You know, it might help us understand the base firefighters' challenges if I flew in one of your jets." The commander smiled, and a call came quickly.

I soon trained and prepared for takeoff in a Kansas Air National Guard F-4 Phantom jet. Before we took off, base personnel took a picture with me beside the jet in full flight suit and helmet regalia. The caption read: "Presented to James Sparr for risking life and limb by flying in an F-4 Tactical Fighter with the intrepid aviators of the Kansas Air National Guard on 4 June 1985."

I proudly displayed that plaque in my home and enjoyed people who asked about my service. I always smiled and told them to reread the caption and finished by telling them I had been part of a great paramilitary organization, the fire service. There's a word in the caption that's interesting: "Tactical." Also on McConnell AFB was SAC, the Strategic Air Command. I mentioned strategy and tactics before.

Part of the training before flight included trouser training. Now, before the mind wanders, let me explain that the flight suit had an inflatable pair of pants with a hose and air connection to the plane. That device inflated and squeezed the legs when the plane was banking or pulling out of a dive. Gravitational pull (g-force) caused physiological reactions. Excessive g-force associated with a steeper pullout forced blood from the upper body, particularly the head, and a flyer could pass out. The pressurized pants forced blood back into the upper body. When g-force subsided, pressure released from the inflated pants.

The jet I flew in stayed in formation with three others to an area in Kansas known as the Smoky Hill Weapons Range. We practiced bombing runs and some aerial maneuvers. When finished, we joined in the formation and flew back to the base. While in the formation I easily saw pilots' and rear-seat passengers' faces in the jets next to our plane. Because the military thought of everything, they also provided barf bags. I didn't use mine but witnessed others doing so. I had seen four jets come in together for a landing many times. The first one landed while others banked off, flew around, and then landed one at a time. That's what we did.

After that experience, I also hitched a ride in the back of a KC-135 tanker. We flew down toward Barksdale AFB, and en route watched a fighter jet refueling. Through the tanker's tail section, we saw a fighter jet maneuver into place and accept the nozzle for refueling. We were so close we could see the pilot's face with an oxygen mask and helmet. The entire training operation fascinated me because that precision maneuvering brought together planning, organizing, managing, and most importantly, communicating. Those four basic functions of management provided an absolute key to any successful operation or manager.

My father served in the US Navy during World War II. His honorable discharge document stated that he served as an Aviation Radioman Third-Class USN. The back of the document had a remarks area with three lines in all caps: "VICTORY RIBBON WORLD WAR II," "AMERICAN AREA RIBBON," and "ASIATIC PACIFIC AREA RIBBON."

I have his picture in uniform, his stripes, the flag from his coffin, and a picture of his ship entering Pearl Harbor. The photo's back has the ship's name. It's difficult to read, but looks like "the USS *Patapsco* (AOG-1)." I don't know much about those ships except that they carried gasoline and contained asbestos. They provided fuel in remote areas for planes. I know his job title, but don't know what he did because, like many veterans, he never talked about his service.

Because part of our jet flight training included emergency ejection and parachuting, I thought about my skydiving adventure in 1980. We trained at the Hutchinson Naval Air Station, not too far from Wichita. A naval air station in the middle of Kansas only made sense because of nearby Wichita. I often wondered if my father took some of his training there, and that's why we ended up in Wichita.

I met our jumpmaster in a local watering hole. The jumpmaster told me what he did for a living. After a couple of my favorite scotches, I proclaimed, "I'm in." Shortly after that my training began. We became familiar with parachutes, packing parachutes, and an emergency parachute. We went over procedures for jumping out of a plane, controlling right and left movements, and controlling our rate of descent, how to land, and where to land.

The instructor had an aerial photograph of the two runways with a taxiway between them that together looked like a giant letter *A* with long legs. The long legs had another grass-worn path between them that paralleled the taxiway between the triangle's base and the end of the long legs. That meant the top part above the paved path formed a triangular grass-covered area, but the lower grass-covered area didn't look like a triangle. The jumpmaster took his long stick with a black rubber tip, pointed to the lower grass area, and in a clear and distinct voice said, "Land in the grassy triangle area." The triangle seemed minuscule compared to the other area the instructor's pointer rested on, but he said "triangle." I always grimaced when some genius in a classroom would note something like "The rubber tip is not resting on the triangle," so I kept quiet. He told us about the dangers of landing on concrete, but that seemed obvious.

After more repetitive instruction and when the ever-present wind subsided, we loaded into a single-engine Wichita-built Cessna aircraft. The pilot did a great job of getting us into position for jumping because he calculated wind speed and knew from experience the proper altitude and position for a successful landing area. I moved into position with a line attached that automatically opened my parachute and, when instructed, jumped. I leaped as far out from the plane as possible because of a warning about becoming entangled and threw both of my arms out. A brief but long-felt moment before my parachute opened caused some free-falling followed by a rather abrupt jerk. That felt reassuring.

After the initial exhilarating jump, the ride down was peaceful. It reminded me of the time I rode in a sailplane and hot-air balloon, only less restrictive. I saw the tiny vehicles below and heard the sounds of tires on pavement and voices from the miniature characters standing on the tarmac. While drifting toward the ground, I adapted and started working a little harder for my target area. The ground person stood in the large grassy open space, waved his hands, and repeated, "Here!" The whole time my positioning focused on the little triangle, as instructed. The ground person began running to the taxiway that formed the triangle's base. I drifted above his head, and made a perfect landing, as instructed.

After regrouping, everyone discussed my handling of the old canopy parachute, a triangle, and that other geometric shape. We finally agreed on continuing the discussions that night at the same watering hole.

That evening the jumpmaster explained my front neck muscle soreness.

"That's the oooooh syndrome. It occurs from the time of initial jump and free-falling until a parachute opens."

The jumpmaster explained, "The corners of the mouth point downward as neck muscles involuntarily tighten, and a voice can only manage an oooooh sound." The only other time I remember hearing that sound came from an audience reaction to my knee popping during the gymnastics competition. The military jet flight and skydiving checked off most of my personal goals except for one—finding the right mate. That would soon change.

Backseat Warrior

25

SEARCH OVER

Because for years I failed at finding a lifelong mate, I began considering a process for analyzing a relationship that began with identifying important personal characteristics. The three main categories of consideration included physical, intellectual, and emotional aspects. The review process went on for thirteen years after my second divorce, so my failure at reaching my ultimate goal didn't result from a lack of effort.

The physical dimension, although viewed differently by individuals, seemed obvious because that's what initially caught one's eye. An emotional connection seemed important because that became the basis for passion. Caution dictated a balance between passion and emotional stability. Finally, the intellect mattered most long term. I analyzed that quality by hearing interesting conversation and humor.

One afternoon, while I was hitting golf balls across the street from my house, a nearby jogger interrupted my practice. After watching her run out of sight, I paused and reflected on the first aspect, physical. Even from two hundred feet away that seemed a no-brainer.

Hair has always been a sensual symbol in literature, and her long brown hair in a French braid swayed rhythmically as she ran. I wondered how long her hair flowed when out of the braid. Her sculpted leg muscles looked great from the side and back as she turned the corner. I thought, *If she passes by again I will invite her to a formal analysis to explore the intellectual and emotional dimensions.*

I told my son about the enchanting woman. A few days later, as Derek sat supervising my efforts in our vegetable garden, he asked, "Is that her?"

I turned around and saw her jogging past our house. Sure enough, she made the mistake of not altering her route, thereby avoiding potential analyzers.

I wore my jogging shorts, sneakers, and a white T-shirt. By the time I rinsed off my hands, she was about two blocks away. I could have sprinted and caught up, but that would have produced labored breathing and not-so-smooth conversation. I grabbed my car keys, jumped in the car, and drove to one-half block behind her. I got out and jogged along beside her.

I introduced myself, told her where I lived, and muttered something about noticing her while practice-hitting golf balls.

"Where do you work?" I asked.

"The Red Cross."

"That's only a couple of blocks from my office at city hall. What's your name?"

"Kelli."

"I apologize for interrupting your run and will leave in a few minutes." I asked if she played golf, and she said no, but she occasionally played tennis.

"Maybe we can play tennis sometime, but would you mind if I call you at work for lunch?" After a few blocks, she probably realized I had enough stamina for tennis.

"Okay." Thank goodness for the fire department physical fitness program.

I called Kelli the next morning, and we set a meeting time for lunch.

I drove from city hall, parked my car in the Fire Station No. 1 lot, and walked next door to the Red Cross building. Kelli stood out front, wearing a pink dress with a rounded wide white collar. Her beautiful face and long flowing hair out of the braid presented a mesmerizing image. As we walked to my car, she appeared somewhat shy, as she had when we first talked, but quickly warmed up when I asked her about our encounter yesterday.

"I was a little apprehensive at first, but when I went home after running, I told my roommate about you and our meeting. We were in the middle of discussing the need to start taking more chances when you appeared on a television interview. I told my roommate, 'That's him.'"

"That was the interview on a fire prevention program."

"Learning you are a fire chief made me feel more comfortable about your invitation this morning."

I truly loved my job. "Well, that makes me more comfortable with the thought that you wouldn't go out with just anyone who asked."

She laughed, and we drove to the art museum for lunch, where volunteers got more people interested in art and also prepared lunch, with proceeds going to the museum. Our lunch conversation went so well, we also met for dinner that evening. The next day Kelli sent flowers to my office, and that caused a bit of a stir among staff but fed my ego. Her inner beauty seemed equal to her physical beauty. She talked a lot about her family, and I easily saw her loyal, emotional family bond.

A true assessment of her emotional landscape came over time, but one day I produced an assessment exercise of my own in the form of musical notes mentioned in chapter 14. That did two things. First, that exercise gave me a lifelong witness to my lesser-known talent, and second, through all that she hung in there.

Her intellect became a little questionable given that she stayed with me, but her sense of humor outweighed that. We've been together now for over thirty-four years. All these years later we still laugh about life's irony, satire, sarcasm, and facetiousness every single day. She's such a lucky woman and knows it, because when I remind her of that, she always says, "Uh-huh." I got lucky because Kelli loved her ornery father and irreverent favorite uncle.

In 1985, Kelli and I took our first ten-hour trip together to Colorado and the Gunnison Valley. I had made that annual pilgrimage the third week in August for over fifteen years, always leaving early in the morning. The morning we left, the red glow of dawn with scattered pink and purple storm clouds gave way to a clear midmorning sky and a quickly warming Kansas summer day. US 54 out of Wichita followed old cattle trails through endless flat wheat fields to Dodge City, the first segment of the journey. That's probably the trail Wyatt Earp took when he left Wichita for Dodge City, only he rode through endless flat prairie land before wheat farming.

A few miles before Dodge City, a small community called Fort Dodge comes into view with a complex of white wood-siding structures. The total complex provides housing and health services for older war veterans. Fort Dodge had served veterans dating all the way back to the Mexican-American and Civil Wars. The most significant history of Fort Dodge centers on the fact that the complex had welcomed veterans from both sides of the Civil War, including black veterans.

A short way out of Fort Dodge, we turned right onto an archway that spanned two sets of railroad tracks, then turned left onto the main highway through Dodge City. The next few blocks had a scattering of small businesses on the right side of the highway with old grain-storage elevators and railroad tracks along the left. Shortly after that is the tourist attraction, Boot Hill Museum, on the right side. That's where they supposedly buried cowboys, as they all wished, with their boots on. Some pointed boot tips stuck out of shallow graves. The term "Hill" describes the slight incline to the museum, one of the higher Kansas elevations. As grown-ups, we all laughed at television shows like *Gunsmoke* when we saw California mountains in the background.

A short way out of Dodge City, US 54 intersects US 50, which continues to Garden City. The pungent smell of cattle feedlots filled the midmorning warming air, like in all other areas with feedlots. Locals call it the smell of money, but some travelers sense it as an unwelcome part of their journey. Kelli and I just laughed, talked about the advantages of being a vegetarian, and turned on the car's interior air circulation feature.

After a few more miles of wheat, milo (grain sorghum), hayfields, cattle grazing lands, and feedlots, the "Welcome to Colorful Colorado" sign appears. Thirty minutes later Lamar marks the halfway point. Just past noon we approached Pueblo and saw the mountains on the western horizon. After a fast-food meal, we continued on the steady mountain incline with more pine trees and aspens filling the mountain views on the way to Cañon City, then Salida. Just outside Salida, the climb to Monarch Pass began, gradual at first until reaching Maysville, a tiny community of cabins for sale or rent. I pointed to the first house on the right, an old Victorian-style structure painted yellow with white trim. A ground-level bay window sat on a corner angle facing the highway. Inside the bay window sat an empty rocking chair.

"For years I've been driving past that house, and no matter what time of day, an old man sat rocking in that chair. He always waved at passing cars. It's just within the past year or so that he hasn't been there." I waved as we drove slowly by and told Kelli I always did that as a tribute to the old man, because that would probably be me someday in my mountain home.

Outside of Maysville, the road grade becomes steeper and speed limits slower. That's when looking at vehicle license tags becomes unnecessary. The "flatlanders" slow down and brake lights come on at every curve. After the Monarch Mountain Lodge, the first passing lane appears. "Now, watch these flatlanders speed up, then slow down when the lane disappears." Sure enough, as we tried passing a first-time Kansan and Oklahoman visitors, they both sped up. I got around them by exceeding the speed limit. "Look back after the passing lane ends."

"They slowed down. Why do drivers do that?"

"I don't know, but it happens on most passing lanes. Even the ones not in the mountains."

We stopped at the top of Monarch Pass on top of the Continental Divide. Kelli commented, "The scent of the pine trees smells so fresh compared to back home." I smiled as I watched her look around with fascination. I had her hooked on the scenery, and we weren't even near the area I wanted for our future home.

We climbed back in the car, put the transmission in a low gear, and began the steep descent passing the Colorado Department of Transportation building that matched the one on the eastern side. Those buildings store the mixture of materials that plow trucks use all winter long to keep the pass open. One more curve and I set the cruise control on sixty-five miles per hour.

As we entered the Gunnison Valley, Gunnison came into view, with red roofs of Western State Colorado University on the right and the airport on the left. A right turn at the main intersection, three more traffic lights, and the final ten miles to Almont lay ahead. Most of the scenery included ranchers' cattle-grazing lands and sparse residential development, with snowcapped West Elk Mountain peaks on the distant horizon. I pointed to the snow on the peaks. "That's how you can tell they had a heavy winter snowfall. The snow won't completely melt before the next one starts in a month or so."

The narrow V-shaped rock opening into Almont was carved years ago by ancient rivers. The Gunnison River flows one hundred feet to the right of the highway. One more curve and we saw the intersection of the Taylor and East Rivers that formed the Gunnison River. I reminded Kelli of the Wichita Indian folklore about a tornado never striking at the confluence of two rivers. She smiled, then commented, "I'll bet a tornado never has or will strike here."

I rolled the power windows down so we could hear the sound of water pouring over rocks. I turned right at the only intersection in Almont, and we pulled into the Three Rivers Resort parking lot. We unpacked our suitcases and settled into a cabin on the river across from my property. Kelli asked how I found this property and patiently sat as I told the story.

After a couple of visits to the area, I began searching for the perfect property. I wanted a permanent residence in Colorado after retirement. My search continued into the 1980s. My first choice was a beautiful little community named Ouray. As usual, I began focusing on basic considerations such as a golf course, a ski area, a hospital, and an airport for transportation needs. Those requirements led me to Lake City, where I vacationed several summers by trailering a dirt bike behind my car and camping in the mountains. The proximity to Gunnison fulfilled my four requirements.

My interest in Lake City heightened while in town for a much-needed shower. Seated downstairs in a local watering hole, I noticed a flyer behind the bar that advertised an evening of chamber music. The bartender laughed when I asked how they could bill a washboard, banjo, and bongo drum as chamber music. He then explained that the select players and conductor included members of the Wichita and Houston Symphonies. I attended the event.

Local folks traded out accommodations for the chosen few musicians' performances. The musicians had a nice vacation area, and the town heard some world-class music. I planned my vacation around that event the next summer. The only problem with Lake City was the time and distance to my four requisites. That eventually led me to Almont, halfway between Gunnison and Crested Butte.

This small, unincorporated Almont area sat in the center of all activities and necessities I considered essential. I turned the corner at the only intersection in Almont, and there hung a "For Sale" sign on a corner lot, so I made an offer subject to survey and riverfront access. The parcel didn't extend to the river, so I purchased an adjacent piece of property. One property line ran down the middle of the Taylor riverbed.

Trees didn't surround the lot, so there was no wildland fire problem. The southwest exposure away from a mountain base ensured a full day of sun, unlike other canyon property. That proved critical in winter.

Kelli and I spent the next few days visiting my favorite spots for hiking and taking pictures. At every stop, I smiled as I watched Kelli soak in the Gunnison Valley beauty like I originally did. The few short days ended, and Kelli was quiet as we packed for our return journey. As we headed to Gunnison for a quick breakfast stop, Kelli finally said, "I can see why you want to live here after retiring. I'm excited about living here too."

The next year I borrowed a friend's camper and spent a couple of days surveying and staking out building corners of my house design. I learned a valuable lesson during those two days in the camper. My life love and best friend didn't like camping out. Kelli defined camping out as no room service. We never camped out again except for one feeble attempt years later on a three-day and two-night stay in a houseboat on Lake Powell that lasted two days and one night.

In the fall of 1986, a contractor poured the foundation. The following year all basic materials lay on-site and in order. I brought several firefighters from Wichita to the job site, and in seven days we framed, roofed, and enclosed the main structure. It was a Colorado contemporary three-story, with log and some river-rock siding. The home had five bedrooms, four baths, a great room for living room/kitchen combination, and recreation room on the lower level. After retirement, I added an attached garage/workshop area and finished the interior of the grandchildren magnet.

I paid all the firefighters who worked on the project and got their expenses out and back as well as accommodations and meals while on-site. Firefighters had an option of being paid an hourly rate or having the opportunity to use the property before we moved in. A couple of smart ones traded out some labor for using the property. Maxi visited almost every year.

During seven days of sunup-to-sundown construction, local folks said they learned a few new words and had never heard such accompanying vocals to a radio playing "All My Exes Live in Texas." I reminded firefighters of the echo effect and how sounds carried in that small natural amphitheater, but they never missed a beat.

26

You Can't Judge a Book by Its Color

During that construction process in the late summer of 1987, someone from Three Rivers Resort came over and gave me a message that requested a return call to a man in Fort Lauderdale. I had met the assistant city manager Pete Witschen earlier that summer when I applied for the Fort Lauderdale fire chief position and participated in an assessment process. I had completed my twenty years of service with Wichita and accomplished every goal set for the department and myself. Kelli and I needed a means of paying for our Colorado residence so we could live comfortably on my retirement and her employment. After I returned the call and some preliminary small talk, Pete asked, "What would it take to persuade you to come to Fort Lauderdale?"

I couldn't consider a couple of offers before then because of the requisite years of service for my pension. The Fort Lauderdale fire chief advertisement appeared, and I applied since the pay fit our needs. My eighteen-year-old son approved of the move because it was Fort Lauderdale. Kelli acquiesced.

The Fort Lauderdale assessment process narrowed candidates down to three outsiders and a couple from inside the department. I researched the community, city manager, and the sincerity about considering someone from outside.

Herman Brice, a fire chief for Miami, confirmed that the city manager seriously wanted someone from outside the city. My information on the city manager came from Howard Tipton, a city manager for Daytona Beach, Florida. I knew Howard from his previous work with the US Fire Administration and National Fire Academy. Howard gave me the thumbs-up on the Fort Lauderdale city manager, and with that endorsement, I applied.

I told the city manager in Wichita, who replaced Gene Denton, of my plans and updated my progress when I returned to Wichita. He was a short man, slightly built, with small hands and a full head of dark-brown hair. As city managers go, he was a good finance director. He spent hours going through the city's 250,000 requisitions and sent many of them back as unnecessary. He smiled and told me one time, "If departments don't resubmit, I guess they didn't need the items after all." Every year he set the budget, then had service levels match the target numbers.

When I told him about my pending move, he said he would help me if I wanted the Lauderdale job. He, no doubt, received pressure from Politician, so my move would benefit both of us. A reliable source told me that Politician had instructed the city manager to "do whatever it takes to get control of the city employees." Politicians, like the one in Wichita, put pressure on city managers because a charter ordinance placed all personnel matters at the discretion of the city manager and prohibited political interference with employee management. Department heads only recommended hiring, promoting, and disciplining employees. When the assistant manager in Fort Lauderdale called for a reference check, the Wichita city manager said, "He can walk on fire and water."

I knew that because the assistant city manager told me so when he called and offered me the Fort Lauderdale position. When he asked what it would take to bring me to Fort Lauderdale, I told him somewhere close to the pay-scale top. We had a brief silence in communication because Pete knew by now that I could insist on the advertised maximum. There was only one thirty-nine-year-old candidate in the country with a master's degree and over seven years of experience in a major metropolitan city. "How quickly can you come to Fort Lauderdale and finalize the contract?" Pete asked.

A couple of weeks later I checked into a hotel not too far from the beach in Fort Lauderdale. The announcement of my selection appeared in the Fort Lauderdale *Sun-Sentinel*. The local firefighters' union had sent me a bouquet in Wichita that contained a bird of paradise flower unique to tropical areas.

The evening before my meeting I took a stroll along the beach. The sky was clear and the sound of the waves crashing on shore drowned out the sound of vehicles passing by. I saw a fire station near the beach on coastal highway A1A, so a brief visit seemed appropriate. I wore a pink shirt and pink shorts because I wore pink long before a pronouncement that only strong men wear pink. Wearing pink was a tribute to my friend Jerry, who helped change how I view people. Finally, wearing pink became my way of telling people who stereotypically classified others by appearance, *Up yours*.

The station was a two-story brick building with typical roll-up doors in front and a side entrance near the Intracoastal harbor. At the station door, a nice young firefighter greeted me and listened to my requested brief tour. He invited me inside and asked me to wait while he got permission. The officer in charge had his shirt unbuttoned and his feet on the desk as he studied a magazine that didn't appear fire related. He looked up from his reading material and gave the okay.

The young firefighter took me to the vehicle bay and gave me an extensive tour, along with a great layman's explanation of the pretty red truck and shiny equipment. When we got to the pump panel, my questions about water tank capacity, gallons per minute pumping capacity, and response criteria made him ask, "Are you a firefighter?"

"I am."

"Where from?"

"A department in the Midwest."

Then a few of his synaptic responses started firing. His open mouth didn't have words for a few seconds.

"Are you from Wichita?"

I don't know if my clothing color stunned him or what, but his disbelief finally came in the form of another question. "Are you our new chief?"

"I am."

"Sir, would you please wait here for a moment?"

All of a sudden firefighters came pouring out from other rooms, and the officer in charge had his shirt buttoned and tucked in. That wasn't necessary because I never once cared about formality or appearance. My focus had always been on substance over appearance, but they didn't know that. We had a pleasant visit before I left and walked over the Seventeenth Street causeway to my hotel.

The next day, after some business with city hall, I went across the street to fire headquarters. The deputy chief of operations greeted me. "I understand you visited the Bahia Mar station last night."

"The crew couldn't have been any more cordial."

The deputy smiled. "I heard you wore pink last night."

"It's nice to see wide open and accurate lines of communication."

I found out later that a union official in Fort Lauderdale called to talk to another union official in Wichita. The Wichita union representative told him they missed me, and three times had to say, "He's not gay." The Wichita union official knew of my favorite colors but was unaware that my analyzing process had ended. I never missed a chance after that to wear pink.

27

WE'RE NOT IN KANSAS ANYMORE

During that initial visit to Fort Lauderdale, Ann and Bruce MacNeil, both active in the union, chauffeured me around, looking for rental property. I met Ann while at the headquarters station the morning after visiting the Bahia Mar station. I had asked the operations deputy, Ron Robson, if any union representative was nearby, so he introduced me to Ann. At our meeting she asked if I'd made living arrangements yet and I told her I planned on searching for a place the next day. I readily accepted her and her husband's offer of help because that would give me an opportunity for employee input from union members.

The following day they drove me to areas they thought might interest me. They asked what my plans were for the department, and I asked about their concerns. I told them that I wanted input from all interested members on how we could strengthen the department before making recommendations. In recent years, as in many paramilitary organizations, fewer members with military experience had entered fire departments. Top-down management didn't interest younger employees without military service, but they appreciated an opportunity for their input. That approach made employees part of the change process and softened resistance in tradition-bound organizations.

Fort Lauderdale required that department heads live inside the city limits, and I knew two firefighters would have familiarity with all parts of the city. After looking at several choices, Ann finally suggested a place near her Executive Airport station. I knew instantly the complex suited our needs and signed a six-month lease.

I chose that new apartment complex because it had a great landscaped view from the back patio. The pond had a water-spray feature that produced soothing sounds and kept the pond water fresh. The pond had an anhinga (snake bird), so named because of its long slender neck that glided above the water's surface when the bird was swimming. Those magnificent animals dived for their prey and almost never missed. They broke the surface, turned their catch headfirst, and swallowed it whole.

When I returned to Wichita, Kelli, Derek, and I prepared for our journey to a new environment. A former firefighter turned truck driver drove his semi loaded with our furniture and trailered vehicles to Fort Lauderdale. Three days later Kelli, Derek, and I flew down and moved into our new accommodations. Kelli liked the view from the patio, and my son liked the nearby pool.

The first few weeks in Florida went well until Thanksgiving. One area of our compatibility stemmed from Kelli's enjoyment of cooking and my pleasure in eating. She, of course, prepared a traditional Thanksgiving meal. The smell of roasted turkey with well-seasoned dressing and a pecan pie filled the apartment. Derek and I watched football. "Okay, it's ready," Kelli called as we sat down for our holiday feast.

Derek and I neared the end of gorging ourselves when I looked up and noticed a small tear in Kelli's eye. Being a naturally sensitive and caring person, I inquired about the cause of her emotional display. That only caused more tears, but she told me, "This is the first time I've been away from my family on either of the two main holidays." The relocation was more difficult for Kelli than for my son or me because she had never been away from her family. Her mother died at a young age, and as a result, Kelli was close to her father. That kind of emotional family bond impressed me. Now over two years in, we both knew this was a comfortable lifetime relationship. I thanked her for her culinary efforts as I always did after every meal.

Later that evening, as we sat in the bubbling outdoor pool, we talked about the beautiful weather compared to the Midwest cold. That softened both of our sorrowful feelings about missed family members. We made a vow that starting with Christmas, we would begin our family tradition of seafood every Thanksgiving and Christmas. That tradition lasted long after Fort Lauderdale.

When our lease ended, I purchased a condominium two blocks from the beach and encountered my first South Florida condo association. In some organizations, the lead sled dog has the best view, so I soon became president. Condo life carried on nicely until one renter had an unapproved party complete with guests parking on the lawn. One vehicle even blocked the gate leading to a lower-level parking facility. The gate repeatedly banged against that vehicle improperly parked in a compact space and burned out the garage door motor.

Things might have proceeded in a civilized manner, but that night, a ringing phone awakened me from a good night's sleep.

After learning of the situation, I called a towing company and requested all available trucks, caught the glassed-enclosed elevator to the ground level, and took command. My hastily donned bathrobe and deck shoes, along with my mussed hair, should've indicated that I was in no mood for negotiations. The vehicle that damaged the garage door motor became the first casualty removed. While on that side of the building, we plucked another full-sized vehicle parked in a compact space. I've always believed in equal opportunity and treatment.

Then I moved around to the complex front and began bringing trucks from a staging area to remove vehicles parked on the front lawn and blocking a "No Parking" sign. As we neared a clean sweep, the beeping noise of backing tow trucks caught the attention of party revelers six stories above. The revelers lined up on an open-air walkway, watching the entertainment below, when one of them commented, "Hey, that's my car."

The party vastly exceeded what would have been a legal occupancy rate in a commercial environment. By then people exited down the stairwells and elevator. My command of the operation succeeded except for a couple of escapees. I returned to my night's rest in anticipation of a regular happy morning.

I found out later that it was an after-party for some benefit. One attendee had a friend on the city council, and I had the attendee's car towed. We exchanged some correspondence related to the definition of a compact car. His political connections didn't impress me. The correspondence ended with my comment that dialogue could continue as soon as he brought me a letter from a local car rental company certifying his car as a compact vehicle. The entire incident made Kelli and me reminisce about midwestern values. Although Wichita had some rude and insensitive folks, most neighbors wouldn't even consider behaving like that. At least they would have followed the rules, controlled their guests' behavior, and apologized the next day for any problems with an offered assistance that made things right. Not in Fort Lauderdale. There existed a rude attitude among a few that others should get out of their way, keep quiet about any problems, and be grateful for their presence. Those few people lived by my old false motto: "Never accept blame when you can pass it along."

Most owners and renters, on the other hand, seemed like pleasant people, and my favorite fellow owner lived next door. Vinny stood slightly over five feet tall with thinning black hair and brown eyes. He walked with a limp because one leg was shorter than the other. We never discussed the cause. It didn't matter anyway because, after a couple of greetings with Vinny's happy smile, the affliction went unnoticed. Vinny had retired as a doorman at a prestigious hotel in New York. That smile, which looked like he had been saving it just for you, probably earned him some good tips.

Since retirement, he occupied much of his time supervising his wife's cooking. Their culinary ritual started midmorning and continued through the day until dinner was served that evening. My favorite weekend days included the roasted garlic smell of a simmering sauce drifting right into our condo when Vinny left his outdoor walkway window open.

I knew that Vinny and his wife's masterpiece neared completion about 4:00 p.m., so I frequently positioned myself on our outdoor walkway overlooking the Intracoastal Waterway. A clear view of Vinny's front door seemed more important than the Intracoastal Waterway. Right on time, Vinny came out onto the open-air walkway for his afternoon cigarette. If he saw me, he did an about-face, went back inside, and reappeared with a nice taster portion on a polished porcelain plate. Every time my praise for their efforts tapered off, Vinny rekindled our conversation with a simple question in his accented English. "Presidente, you like?"

"Yes, Vinny, as usual, it's the best." That parting smile always appeared.

28

A HORSE TOO FAR

Although we had some difficulty adapting to our surrounding culture, the first two months of settling in at the Fort Lauderdale Fire Department were easy because of knowledgeable staff. By the second month at work, I called for a planning session and charted the department's future course. Attendees included all chief ranking officers and the office manager. I used a simple brainstorming exercise that elicited ideas on what the department needed for moving forward. We filled at least two flip-chart sheets of paper.

I assigned twenty-one committees the task of making recommendations for implementing suggested changes and placed two requirements on each committee. They must include a member from each rank, and committees must provide periodic reporting until completion. I concluded the session by announcing, "The train's leaving the station and everyone's welcome aboard, but if anyone is unhappy for whatever reason, you're also welcome to stay behind."

The time came for addressing the rank and file via video regarding the department's future direction and what each of our roles and responsibilities should be in the forward progress. I chose a visual image from my younger days.

The department had a professional video-training section headed by a phenomenal officer nicknamed Lieutenant Video. Firefighters always anticipated his training videos because of the interesting side comments or music he added. Most of his videos opened with a scene of fire and smoke accompanied by a line from Lynyrd Skynyrd's "That Smell."

With the scene set behind our training station under the chin-up bar, I provided a simple script. I chose the biggest and most ornery firefighter because he had a shaved head and looked like a cross between a gang biker and Mr. Clean. We met at the training facility. The scene called for him to sit on my shoulders while I gave a brief speech about our future direction. By then my forty-year-old injured knees made squat lifting difficult. The plan had Mr. Clean grabbing hold of the chin-up bar and assisting in raising the *Titanic*.

I gave Lieutenant Video instructions on focusing in and eliminating the chin-up bar as Mr. Clean folded his arms across his chest while perched on my shoulders. We had a little difficulty because Mr. Clean had a wrist as bad as my knee.

I finished the speech by saying, "If you carry your load, I will support you and carry my load." After the video was shown, I'm not sure the firefighters got the message because they kept harassing Lieutenant Video. They wanted answers about the trick he had used to seat Mr. Clean. To paraphrase a previous statement, directors sometimes get too caught up in visual images and lose the message. Later, we produced a much less intense farewell video with a clearer message.

Fire departments across the country are similar in many ways, but there are cultural differences. In Fort Lauderdale one of those differences became clear. Our safety program also included a review of all accidents (mistakes), stating who did what and how similar accidents (mistakes) could be prevented. I was used to people like Loudy, who admitted what had occurred, and I appreciated the interjection of humor. My values, formed in the Midwest, differed from some in South Florida. Like some of the condo folks, few admitted their part in any mistakes, and mitigating circumstances like temporary memory loss popped up out of nowhere.

I instituted a policy of discipline that included less or no punishment if complete honesty became part of the equation. I proposed that concept during an individual's hearing for discipline, and the union attorney called for a caucus. The attorney came back and asked privately, "Are you serious about lesser or no punishment? He thinks you're going to fire him if he admits his part in a cover-up attempt."

"I am serious."

The union attorney sold the deal. Of all the private practice attorneys I dealt with in South Florida, Bob Klausner seemed the best because he always tried reaching a compromise rather than waste union money. That's when I took to saying, "When all else fails, tell the truth."

One of the programs we began was for physical fitness. I again tried improving the health and safety of firefighters. That fitness program was less intense than Wichita's because it didn't include benchmark testing.

Firefighters requested a nonsmoking policy, which made negotiations with the union easier. The Benevolent Association and union collaborated with the University of Miami and produced a smoke-free-workplace poster for fire and police. I gave permission for the use of fire department images. The poster had of one of our fire lieutenants in firefighting gear with a little soot on his face. In the picture, from his chest up, he had a lit cigarette in his mouth with smoke pouring out of the corner of his lips. The caption read, "The deadliest fire is right under your nose." Part of our program included a nonsmoking policy in the stations, and not long after city hall caught up.

We also initiated the incident command system (ICS). The success of ICS depended on dispatchers doing their part since a key element of the system involved communication. We had dispatchers dedicated to fire department dispatching only, and we made them feel like a part of the fire department family.

Fire prevention was always one of my key concerns in promoting firefighter safety. We had seventeen personnel dedicated to fire prevention, and two other key elements in our fire prevention program. One, the South Florida building codes, had a county edition for Palm Beach, Broward, Dade, and Monroe Counties. The other, a Board of Rules and Appeals, had contractor and fire officer members. Our fire marshal sat on that board as a voting member. That meant the board strongly supported code enforcement.

Fire prevention personnel pursued a sprinkler retrofitting program for high-rise buildings like we did in Wichita. The retrofitting program required the issuance of building permits. After my third year in Fort Lauderdale, the building official informed me that our retrofitting program accounted for over 70 percent of the dollar value of all building permits issued.

When I arrived in 1987, over twenty different fire departments operated in Broward County, which had an organization called the Broward County Fire Administrators. Ray Briant, from the city of

Tamarac, presided over the organization. Ray was the first person outside of Fort Lauderdale who welcomed me to South Florida. Ray, like a lot of residents, originally came from New York City. He was a former member of the FDNY. He convinced me to take over as president of the administrators' organization.

The chiefs of member departments broke into different committees and provided monthly reports on progress. One committee oversaw the administration of our mutual aid agreements. I thought the operative word in mutual aid should be "mutual." Larger departments aided smaller departments with little in return. The fire response was a generally accepted practice, but specialty responses, like hazardous materials spills, were another matter.

Communities like Fort Lauderdale invested thousands of dollars in special vehicles, equipment, and training, so the Broward County Fire Administrators instituted a fee for hazardous materials response. All but one city, whose councilmen all exceeded the age of seventy, agreed on the fee. I complained to Ray one day in our monthly meeting about the seventy- and eightysomething councilmen of that particular city. With a smile on his face, Ray jokingly said, "I understand because their parents live in my community. Just send them a letter making the consequences clear if they don't agree."

Another issue in some of those local communities was the lack of knowledge and training on ICS. Larger departments didn't want to place their firefighters under the command of untrained and inexperienced officers. Someone suggested that we send them a notice that they had a few weeks for certified training on ICS, or they would no longer receive mutual aid. The notices went out to two noncompliant cities, addressed to their city administrators. Not long after that, I received a copy of a memo from a Fort Lauderdale councilman to our city manager asking about my authority to mandate such harsh requirements.

My response through channels read, "I acted as a spokesperson for the Broward County Fire Administrators, not our fire department." I added a suggestion that the councilmen review the mutual aid agreement. The agreement let fire professionals administer the agreement, thereby eliminating political interference. A phone call followed the memo, reminding everyone of the consequences of political interference with public safety officials. Sanctions included a possible fine, jail time, and removal from office. I didn't hear another word on that subject.

When it came time for retrofitting city hall with sprinklers, the councilman asked, "What are you going to do if we don't?"

"I will take the city before the Board of Rules and Appeals."

He claimed he had a legal opinion that governmental immunity precluded that. Wrong! Governmental immunity applied only if government officials followed professional advice. The real municipal attorneys upstairs later confirmed that. Unlike the one in Wichita who would compromise public safety, the Florida politician seemed more like a humorous, pesky fly that occasionally needed shooing away.

29

THE ALPHA-DOG SYNDROME

By 1988, safety became a larger part of our organizational culture as we prepared specifications for our first new fire truck. I instructed the color to be lime yellow. There was much wailing and gnashing of teeth. Some used the poor little conjunction *but* excessively and improperly. I pointed to definitive and empirical studies by Dr. Stephen S. Solomon. The objectors pointed to comments made by relatives who thought red a better color. One said he thought flashing lights made colors irrelevant.

"You thought, but what did you used to think? What about when the lights aren't on?"

Here it came again: "The public is familiar with red trucks, and that makes red more noticeable."

I applied a "how to think" question of reasoning to that "what to think" statement. "Shouldn't the color be unfamiliar, therefore more noticeable? There's a reason why football teams don't use their familiar team colors on goalposts."

The naysayers had a contrarian councilman bring the issue up in a city council meeting. When nothing happened, we ordered a new truck. I preferred red, but my safety commitment didn't end with the color of fire vehicles. As in Wichita, I had an open-door policy with the right to speak freely on any subject. Change agents elicited strong positive and negative opinions. One union representative came in and posed a simple question that I'd also heard in Wichita. "Doesn't it bother you that people hate you?"

"No, because I don't come to work to be loved. I go home for my loving. I come to work to keep you safe."

Three years later, the firefighters had a panoramic picture taken with their three new pumpers, three new Suburbans, a new hazmat vehicle, and a new aerial—all in that unfamiliar color, with a note that read, "Thanks." When the time came for ordering a new Executive Airport firefighting vehicle, the Federal Aviation Administration, as with all airports, mandated a yellow color—*hmm*.

Each year the Benevolent Association handed out awards for extraordinary events that took place the previous year. I particularly enjoyed one award because of an accident (mistake) at the headquarters station, which also housed my office.

The ladder truck always parked behind the pumper at Station 1. Sometime during the night, an alarm came in and the pumper responded. The ladder truck, driven by Herbie Blabon, followed behind the pumper. Both trucks had overhead garage door opener/ closers. That's where things became a little confusing. Either a garage door closer in the pumper, by itself, thought the ladder truck wouldn't be responding, or a garage door opener in the ladder truck watched the door closing and thought the ladder truck should be responding. The ladder truck ripped an all-steel roll-up door from its hinges and sent that door sailing across the street. Damage similar to that had occurred before, but never had a door sailed so far, and that became the basis for an award.

Herbie sat in a chair across from my desk when I arrived the morning after the accident (mistake). He quickly told the whole truth as he knew it, mixed with attempts at humor. I wouldn't admit it then, but Herbie was my favorite. He tried pulling pranks on me that usually backfired, like the time he came into my office for his service award wearing his hat sideways and sporting a goofy pair of glasses. A multicolored hat with a propeller, given to me as a mocking gag gift after I changed the color of the fire trucks, sat on a shelf. I immediately donned it, clasped his hand, and gave the goofiest Stan Laurel smile I could muster.

Another time Herbie put a lifelike rubber snake in my office chair and waited down the hall. I grabbed the tail, but it didn't move. I took the rubber snake and started for the city manager's department-head meeting. Herbie, with a wry grin on his face, asked, "Where are you going with my snake?"

"I'm taking this to the city manager and will tell her what you did."

The smile disappeared as I strolled casually across the lawn, ignoring his calls: "Hold on. Wait a minute."

I did take the rubber snake to the meeting, placed it in manager Connie Hoffman's chair, and sat down next to her. Just then, she entered the room, pulled the chair out, and gasped. I grabbed the snake instantly, proclaiming my ignorance of it not being real.

"I would take a bullet or snakebite for you anytime."

The police chief shook his head and rolled his eyes. I stuck my tongue out at him. The one-hour meeting produced some anxiety for Herbie until I told him the truth. Herbie also received numerous acknowledgments for rescuing cats. He rescued so many that firefighters accused him of carrying a throw-down cat.

In addition to their extraordinary-events awards, the Benevolent Association occasionally had a look-alike contest. One year they chose me as a winner of the Pat Boone look-alike contest. A talented retired member, Tom Crews, drew a caricature of the look-alike along with some identifying personal touches.

These included a caricature of an autographed picture of Clint Eastwood that hung on my office wall, with a caption that read, "Love, Clint." He also drew an image of a fire truck, naturally painted yellow, hanging next to Clint's picture. He added little musical notes with words from a Pat Boone song. I gave them my musical rendition of those opening words when they presented my award.

The drawing also had a "No Smoking" symbol, a book titled *Physical Fitness*, and I wore a pair of sneakers with my feet on the desk. Tom nailed it. A nameplate with "Chief Jim Sparr Wichita, Kansas," stuck out of the trash can.

The nameplate in the trash came about because I instructed staff that if I mentioned Wichita, they should respond, "Where?" They never asked the question because of anything I said. One of my many pet peeves was someone who always said, "Well, back in such and such a place we used to . . ."

I always responded, "If it's so great, why aren't you still there?"

As for the sneakers, I started wearing them with my suits years earlier in Wichita and now with casual clothing. My normal Fort Lauderdale attire included a golf shirt with city logo, slacks, and deck shoes or sneakers. Our city manager at the time, Connie Hoffman, left in 1991. She asked if I needed anything before she departed, and I quickly answered, "Place the informal dress into my contract."

When asked why, I replied, "You never know whom your replacement might be."

A reporter for the newspaper, encouraged by firefighters, once asked me why Connie allowed my casual dress.

"Connie, like me, concerns herself more with substance through job performance than appearance." That ended that interview.

Sure enough, we got a three-piece-suit manager (too nice for South Florida politics that, like the anhinga bird, sometimes swallowed its prey whole). I'm sure a politician made him ask me, at the end of my yearly evaluation, about the possibility of wearing a suit, as I had at commission meetings.

"No."

"Why?"

"It's in my contract." Anytime he heard something he didn't like he shifted to one side in his seat, and his responding sentence grew higher in pitch. I had already figured out the reason for a higher pitch. When he shifted in his chair, he must've put more pressure on one of his testicles. He asked in that southern drawl, "Een your CONtract?"

"Yes," I said, and returned across the street to my office.

A few minutes later I received a call from the best municipal attorney on staff, Linsey Payne. She asked, "Are you having difficulty with the manager?"

"No, why?"

Linsey said the manager wanted a copy of my contract. She laughed when I told her the story. Anticipation and planning were important in life.

Anytime a new manager took over any organization, they engaged in what I called "the alpha-dog syndrome." That's to say, they announced their presence by marking their territory. The difference between individuals was shown via markings of appearance or substance. Appearance-oriented managers used markings to say, "I'm the boss now." My marking included lime-yellow trucks and the substance of safety.

After leaving, Connie Hoffman went to the private sector. She eventually returned to public service as town manager for Lauderdale-by-the-Sea, Florida. Good for them. I felt honored and privileged working for her because she focused on teamwork and employee well-being.

Herbie's Service Award

Look-A-Like Award

30

PRANKING RULES

The previously mentioned Baggers were my national networking group, while the Broward County Fire Administrators became my local one. All the chiefs came up through the ranks with verbal volleyball and pranks that seemed like a natural part of professional relationships. I met not only Ray Briant but two other fire chiefs who became good friends of mine: Huey Manges, fire chief for Port Everglades, and Jim Ward, fire chief for an adjacent city, Hollywood, Florida.

Huey, a stoutly built man, had thinning dark hair that he parted two inches above his right ear. He always wore a suit with a crisply laundered shirt and brightly polished leather shoes. Every time we met, he looked me up and down, shook his head disapprovingly, and said, "I don't know how you get by with dressing like that."

"My boss, unlike yours, is more concerned with job performance." I then followed with "You should appreciate me more because I am your clothing *Picture of Dorian Gray*. I make even you look good."

Huey had a good friend in the sheriff's office who took us for a helicopter ride when I first arrived in Fort Lauderdale. My operations deputy told me of the arrangement, and that Huey would fly with us. That had significance because Huey feared flying. We all boarded the helicopter with Deputy Ron and "Baby Huey" in the back seats. I told the pilot about my flying experience and asked about climbing into the left front pilot's seat. Before he could say no, Huey protested loudly and indicated he wanted out until I climbed into the right front seat. I found the flying experience informative and exhilarating, but Huey had his eyes closed most of the time.

Baby Huey, as I nicknamed him, and I met almost every late Friday afternoon at the Old Florida restaurant for a drink. The main bar was separated from the dining area because of compliance with Florida's Clean Indoor Air Act regarding smoking in public places. The bar had a large oval-shaped top with a bartender's well in the oval's middle. A few tall tables and stools lined the wall. The main bartender, Flip, had a handsome, youthful appearance, with blue eyes and curly hair. He walked with a slight limp because of a motorcycle accident. Huey chain-smoked but tried giving it up when we started our No Smoking program. He used patches as his method of quitting. One afternoon in Old Florida, Huey and I stood at the end of the bar as Huey flicked his cigarette ashes near the giant ashtray Flip provided. Flip cleaned the bar and ashtray with a damp cloth, then set the ashtray back in front of Huey. "I thought you quit smoking."

"I'm cutting back with the help of patches." Huey opened his shirt, revealing not one but three patches.

I asked Flip, "Did Huey tell you about the cruelty-to-animals inquiry?"

"No, but I'd love to hear about it."

"Our mutual acquaintance, Charley Rule, pulled a little prank on Huey. Remember the recent fire in a warehouse on the Port Everglades property?" Flip nodded in agreement. "The firefighters directed an extinguishing agent into the warehouse with a Mack fire truck. During that operation, paint on the truck's front blistered, and an ornamental Mack bulldog on the hood sustained discoloring. After someone provided details, Charley sent Huey a pretend message from the ASPCA, wanting a full accounting regarding the bulldog's cruel treatment."

Huey then asked, "Are you the one who sent Charley the information about that bulldog?"

"Would I do that?"

Flip answered Huey's question. "Yes." I can still hear that infectious laugh of Huey's.

Another fire chief friend, Jim Ward, from Hollywood, was one of the first paramedics certified in the state of Florida; he had a model paramedic operation. He teased me about not having ambulances, and I teased him about not having the best firefighting force. Of course, that held no truth, but when an opportunity presented itself, I said, "Don't pass it up." One day at an administrators' meeting, a newspaper picture circulated the room. The picture showed a ladder truck pouring water into the roof of a small house that had been on fire. I inquired as to exactly how they extinguished the fire from the building's outside and then I stood back. Our fellow fire chiefs, including Huey, handled the remaining questions. We used pride and humor when discussing serious issues, and all three agreed to continue the pranking discussion after work.

Jim joined Huey and me that Friday afternoon at Old Florida, and we took up the earlier conversation about firehouse pranks. Jim told us one of the best gotcha stories. As he explained, not long after the Florida lottery started, one shift of firefighters played the numbers together. After a nightly drawing, an oncoming shift firefighter stopped and bought a ticket that matched the previous day's winning numbers. He got into a locker and slipped the ticket into a stack of numbers, fixed a cup of coffee, and sat back to witness the happy celebration. Disbelief carried over when the crew went off duty. They proceeded to the place of ticket purchase, and a heated discussion ensued until the store owner pointed out the date of purchase on the ticket. Jim said, "I never heard the story about retaliation, but I'm sure something happened."

As a young man working at Boeing, I observed how a sense of pride and use of humor helped build successful work groups. In Fort Lauderdale, pranking continued both inter-departmentally and intra-departmentally. A favorite prank happened after one of the many entertainment opportunities available in and near the city. A member of my favorite band, Joe Walsh of the Eagles, was born a "Wichita boy." The Eagles broke up, and band members went their separate ways. One of the founding members, Don Henley, toured for his *End of the Innocence* album. Don booked three consecutive nights at a nearby venue.

I occasionally played golf on weekends with a guy who mentioned he could arrange for a backstage pass. I purchased tickets for all three nights, and when I went to the ticket booth, an attendant handed me a backstage pass. After the concert, I briefly met with Don and gave him a note that listed the times and places of all his concerts I had attended. The note ended with "I will see you next time."

Don wrote on the note, "To Jim, thanks for your support over all these years," and signed it. Don, like Clint Eastwood, impressed me the first time I saw him display his craft. Don's lyrical poetry fascinated me, and when I heard his voice it cemented my status as a starstruck fan. I also liked his boldness and honesty. When asked, he never hesitated to give his opinion. I missed a chance for a picture with Roy Orbison, who performed at a Darryl Starbird Rod and Custom Car Show in Wichita and always regretted that. Don granted my request for a picture the next night and signed the photograph the following night. That picture hung on a wall of my office next to Clint's autographed picture. One day, some firefighters came into my office and photocopied my portion of the picture with Don Henley. They flattered me because it seemed they only wanted my picture until I learned why they'd reproduced it.

The fire-prevention-minded firefighters produced a short public safety film on Christmas trees and fire potential. Firefighters built a small room containing a dry Christmas tree, some wrapped gifts, and my picture on the wall. The firefighters simulated an electrical fire, and the fire took off rapidly. Of course, Lieutenant Video filmed the entire event and kept focusing on my picture, hoping the flames of hell would consume the evil person who insisted on lime-yellow fire trucks.

The fire consumed the entire structure, and firefighters doused remaining embers. The picture landed facedown on the ground; when they retrieved their burned effigy, my smiling face stared back at them. Before that event, my nickname was Chief Reebok. They even had a pair of Reebok fire boots made up as a gag gift. Now it became Chief Mercury because, like the chemical element, anytime they tried putting their finger on me, I squirted away. I didn't get the metaphor but smiled and said, "Maybe you should quit fingering me." One of them commented to another, "No matter what happens, he's always watching and smiling."

Soon afterward a fluke picture confirmed their observations. I started a tradition of having my picture taken with firefighters on every ten-year anniversary of a firefighter's service. I gave them a brief speech about how much we appreciated their years of service. A small ship porthole with a mirror in the center hung on a wall in my office. If we stood just right, my reflection also appeared in the mirrored porthole, thereby proving that I was not a bloodred-sucking vampire. Naturally, we replicated that picture every time.

A corroborating event regarding my ever-presence occurred when two of our National Guard firefighters headed out for Operation Desert Shield. The logistical captain helping with their processing asked a confirming question: "Are you both Fort Lauderdale firefighters?"

They looked at each other, and then answered, "Yes, Captain, why do you ask?"

"Because I know your fire chief would want me to tell you to be safe."

Here they stood, miles away from Lauderdale, but had no idea that Lee, a PGA instructor, and I met in Fort Lauderdale. She tried but couldn't improve my golf swing. My only regret about Fort Lauderdale was that we left before I could attend a formal military ball as Lee's escort. Kelli originally agreed with my escort offer because, while Lee fought a losing battle with my golf swing, she succeeded in delivering my safety message to firefighters.

There arose some question about continuing the guardsmen's pay status while overseas. I told staff who remained in contact with the guardsmen I would win that battle. The guardsmen should focus on their safety.

31

MISSION ACCOMPLISHED

My son, Derek, lived with me until he turned twenty-one. I told him that if he ever got into trouble, he should never use my name and position to help him out. The original instruction came in Wichita when a police radar officer caught him exceeding the speed limit and saw his last name, and Derek readily confirmed that the fire chief was his father.

That radar officer, Jackie Gates, let him go, and I didn't find out about it until a few days later when she smiled and mentioned it while in an elevator in city hall. We both laughed, but I politely asked her to not do that again should the occasion arise. That evening my instruction came with a promise that some form of discipline would follow if he dropped my name and position again.

Hundreds of miles and a number of years apparently dulled his memory. I awoke late one night from a phone call activated from the downstairs intercom. Two of Fort Lauderdale's finest asked for a parental conference. I dressed and caught the elevator, and one officer greeted me while the other stood guard over the perpetrator, who had his hands on the police cruiser's trunk lid.

The officer explained they had just caught him drinking beer on the beach, and they wanted him released to my custody rather than taking him to jail. I first asked, "Was he cooperative?" and the officer replied yes.

"Did he mention my position?"

The officer replied yes, to which I said, "Take him to jail."

The officer took me out of my son's hearing range. "We're going off duty and don't want to do all of the paperwork." After confirming it truly had nothing to do with my position, they released Derek to my custody. On the elevator, we discussed his need for other living arrangements. "You're twenty-one now, so starting tomorrow, search for other living arrangements. You may need one month's deposit, so don't pay me this month's rent."

"Okay, thanks."

We relived those fun times after an event in 2012. I traveled to Wichita and gave the keynote speech for an awards ceremony. I met with the fire chief and management staff that morning before the evening's event. One of the top management staff relayed a story about the time, before joining the WFD, she taught my son at North High School. He had some difficulty with the subject matter and asked her if she knew his dad, the fire chief. Derek told her that he would be in peril if he took a bad grade home. That was untrue given my poor academic record. To her credit, she told him that a little extra hard work would probably help. Upon arrival back in Colorado, I called him, and we had a good laugh about both incidents.

That chief officer mentioned one other thing: "I'm grateful to the women who went before me." I thought about her comment after leaving the building. She later climbed to the top rung of the organizational ladder. Under her leadership, Wichita got a class 1 rating for fire defense. That rating potentially saves commercial building owners significant sums of money on fire insurance rates.

Except for female minorities, the opposition to women entering the fire service couldn't compare to racial integration, but I'm sure women endured inappropriate comments and behavior. Some male firefighters wouldn't admit that women could do their jobs. Some old Fort Lauderdale badges still had "FIREMAN" embossed on them. One firefighter retired and passed his badge on to a younger firefighter, who thought it was funny teasing women firefighters with his badge. After someone complained to me, I confiscated the badge. That issue never came up again. In some departments, the women's auxiliary voiced opposition with questions about sleeping attire and the privacy of bunking. One fire chief in a major Wisconsin city commented on a national morning news program in the 1980s, "Women don't belong in the fire service. They can't do the job like a man can." He survived continued employment because he had a lifetime appointment.

In Fort Lauderdale, several women—including Ann MacNeil, who gave me my initial real-estate tour—had already joined the fire department. I purposely don't remember how many because that was a question I resented hearing. *How many do you have?* sounded like quantity mattered more than qualifications. I usually responded, "All of our firefighters are fully qualified; some just happen to be women." That response also blunted an occasional statement: "She only has her job because she's a woman." I attended a conference for Women in the Fire Service in Asheville, North Carolina, with some of our women firefighters, at their request. One guest lecturer found the numbers question offensive because to her it sounded like "How many have infected your department?" We all laughed but knew what she meant.

I announced my retirement before the spring of 1993. Lieutenant Ramsey (Lt. Video) and I produced my farewell video. In addition to the initial brainstorming session in 1987 with managers, we sent out a memo asking all rank and file employees for their suggestions regarding the department's future. That gave everyone a chance for providing input. We set the video scene with my feet on the desk as usual and turned the pages of all the original suggestions for change. Although there were many, on the video I read a partial list of some departmental accomplishments:

1. First responder program and better EMS delivery with a commander in charge
2. Rescue and dive team
3. Publications in national journals
4. Increased media coverage
5. Increased public education demonstrations
6. Hazardous materials vehicle with a commander in charge
7. Physical fitness program and equipment
8. Educational incentives
9. Open-door policy
10. No double standard for discipline
11. Newer equipment and vehicles
12. Increased hands-on training
13. Specialty pay
14. Computer-aided dispatch with dedicated dispatchers
15. Incident command system with standard operating procedures
16. Allowed members to wear their fire department T-shirts when off duty

Only the last one needs a little explanation. I approved a policy of letting firefighters wear their fire department T-shirts when off duty with certain restrictions. One day I saw one of our fighters wearing our department T-shirt with sleeves cut off and cut down the sides because that was a trend. I sent out a memo to all personnel dated August 15, 1988. The short memo read:

One of the things I have observed in my twenty-one years in the fire service is a truism that goes like this: whatever you can find to give firefighters, some will find a way to screw it up. . . . There have been two observances of the latest trend of ripping a perfectly good T-shirt down the sides so that one's titties are visible.

I wrote that my son did the same thing, and I had nothing personal against the practice, except for how it represented the fire department to the general public. I concluded by writing that if self-policing didn't work I would take more stringent action. That infamous memo became known as the "titty memo." The union president Greg Gurdak laughingly said, "You should've used the word 'teats.'"

I replied, "Having milked twenty head of cattle, or eighty teats, twice daily, that term only applies to females. Men are the problem. One of them said that T-shirt ripping was something the women couldn't do. That was my attention-getting way of saying, 'Oh no you can't.'"

At the next department-head meeting, the police chief, who liked playing verbal volleyball, said, "Your secretary should've caught it before sending it out."

"In the Midwest, we accept responsibility for our actions."

Then it came to me, and I turned to the police chief. "You're still sore because of the observation I made in our last budget workshop."

The assistant city manager, Pete Witschen, asked, "Which extreme observation?"

"The one where I told the truth about fire departments that have successfully reduced fire occurrence and death rates and receive budget cuts. Whereas police departments have failed in their mission at reducing crime rates, so in typical government style we will reward their failed efforts by putting more donut-eaters on the street."

The police chief smiled. "Sticks and stones." He then said, "If I remember correctly, you're the one who first recommended more patrol officers."

"I had a weak moment."

The city manager shook her head and proclaimed we needed to move on.

Connie didn't question my management style or techniques, but she did concentrate on results. She told me she had some doubt in the beginning about the prospect of accomplishing such an aggressive agenda, but her confidence grew as she watched success after success. All the firefighters contributed to departmental accomplishments, but one in particular, Tom Weber, stood out and deserved one good story.

Tom and his wife, Mary, tried having children for a long time and finally resigned themselves to the impossibility. Tom came into my office one day and asked if I would like to see their new baby. I thought they had adopted, but actually they'd purchased a new Corvette. Not long afterward, Mary became pregnant, which doctors described as a miracle. The miracle became three miracles, all girls. The Corvette soon gave way to a minivan. I considered those triplets part of my family, and still call them my three angels. They call me Charlie.

Tom held a master's degree in public administration, an accredited chief fire officer designation from the Center for Public Safety Excellence, and an executive fire officer designation from the National Fire Academy. After Tom retired from Fort Lauderdale, he competed for and secured a position as a fire chief in Manchester, Connecticut. Later he became a fire chief in Port Orange, Florida. His excellence in management was recognized by fellow chiefs when they voted him as Florida's fire chief of the year and as president of the Florida Fire Chiefs' Association, and his department as EMS provider of the year. I knew of his talents because we worked together on several consulting engagements.

During one of our phone visits, Tom explained his newest endeavor. He had joined the Insurance Services Office (ISO) team. ISO, a subsidiary of Verisk, rated fire departments, water departments, and dispatch systems. They then provided a fire rating from 1 to 10 for any given community. That final rating became the basis for determining homeowner fire insurance premiums. Tom became the national director of Community Hazard Mitigation for ISO. ISO works to foster an active relationship with fire departments, building departments, water suppliers, and communities. Verisk is a leading source of information about risk. Drawing on vast experience in data management, security, and predictive modeling, Verisk helps clients protect people, property, and financial assets in the United States and around the world.

Rhoda Mae Kerr was another Fort Lauderdale fire department member who achieved impressive credentials and appointments. I recommended Rhoda Mae for promotion to battalion chief and assigned her to the all-important training division. She later became a division chief and retired as a deputy chief, then became a fire chief for Little Rock, Arkansas, before moving on to become the chief in Austin, Texas. In 2018 Chief Kerr returned home and became Fort Lauderdale's fire chief.

Chief Kerr held a master's in public administration, certifications from Harvard's Senior Executives in State and Local Government program, and graduated from the Executive Fire Officer Program. Chief Kerr became president of the Metropolitan Fire Chiefs and president of the International Association of Fire Chiefs. She also sat on the National Infrastructure Advisory Council, which advises a sitting president on matters regarding the security of critical infrastructure and related information systems. I had the privilege of serving with the best fire service representatives who became role models, such as Rhoda, Tom, and others.

Many members of both the Wichita and Fort Lauderdale departments became fire chiefs for other departments. At various times, members from both departments became fire chiefs in Arkansas, Colorado, Connecticut, Florida, Kansas, Missouri, Oklahoma, Texas, and other states. Some of them have thanked me for my help, but I always replied, "Although I am proud of your accomplishments, you are singularly responsible for any achievement. I only provided support and opportunities, like those given to me. You made the most of any opportunity."

I also shielded employees who worked for me from any abuse by instructing office staff in both departments to never take verbal abuse, but rather to direct those people to me. Not long before leaving Fort Lauderdale, a citizen who lived across the street from one of our fire stations called to complain about noisy sirens. Previous cooperation with that guy had worked, but he now threatened one of our staff members with his lawyer.

After hearing his bluster, I recounted how we tried working with him, but for safety's sake, we were rethinking the policy of waiting until a block from his house before activating the siren. I then made it clear that we didn't respond well when threatened, so "Let's put your lawyer against our concerns for safety and see what happens." Before slamming the phone down, I commented, "Don't ever call and threaten us again, or better yet, never call again."

Then my loud voice ended with "If you ever call again, I will have our firefighters lean on the air horns and run sirens at full tilt every time they leave the station." I think he became brand-new, because I don't think he ever called again. Smart move on his part, because by now firefighters knew the location of the bloody spot on the chicken.

After I announced my retirement, the union gave me a T-shirt with sides cut out. The Benevolent Association gave out gold-plated axes with red lettering on the handle next to a red Maltese cross. My ax seemed more special than any previously presented because of the Maltese cross's lime-yellow color. That ax remains on display above my desk. In the evening, when the light dims, I can see the Maltese cross from across the room. I wouldn't be able to see it if the Maltese cross had red paint.

The Broward County Fire Administrators gave me a wooden engraved plaque with an inscription: "In appreciation for your leadership, wisdom, and guidance as President . . ." That plaque remains on display in my workshop.

I used some vacation time and left before any planned party. When I had retired in Wichita, I also called the mayor, thanked him for his support, and told him that I wouldn't appear before the city commission for my service award because firefighters and staff accomplished the real work. I merely had the honor of facilitating change.

With one exception, I've never been afraid of anything or anyone. The only fear I've known focused on a thought that someone under my command might die in the line of duty. Other than the Bethel Baptist Church fire mentioned earlier, the biggest scare occurred in Wichita when a fire truck ran over Lieutenant Max Rhoades. The pumper came into a fire scene too quickly and couldn't stop in time. The truck struck Max and knocked him down, and a front tire rolled over his midsection.

Deputy Chief Campbell and I went to the emergency room and checked on him. Once again, in the absence of information, the mind makes things up. On the way to the hospital, I imagined all kinds of things. When we entered an examination room, Max lay on his back with his hands behind his head, smiling. He showed us the marks on his front midsection and said he had no broken bones or internal damage. He then added, "It's all due to a good physical fitness program."

After I announced my retirement in Wichita and upcoming move to Fort Lauderdale, a television reporter who interviewed me asked me to name my proudest accomplishment.

"No firefighter was mortally wounded under my command, and I left a safer community behind."

For years that same reporter, Gary Shapiro, has been a morning co-anchor in Denver, Colorado. I thought about my response every time I saw Gary, and I felt the same way when leaving Fort Lauderdale.

32

DOWN MEMORY LANE

I purchased a trailer and loaded all our furniture for the Colorado trip. Kelli and I left Fort Lauderdale early one morning in February of 1993 and headed to Colorado via Arkansas, and of course Wichita. Florida's length let us talk about all the things we experienced during the last five and a half years.

One of our favorite visiting places was the Florida Keys. We enjoyed Key West and the colorful characters both present and past. I enjoyed visiting the Hemingway house and Captain Tony's, where he hung out. It was a dingy and not-well-lighted place where some literary characters probably originated. The Keys' temperate winter climate was probably one reason why my favorite president, Harry Truman, liked the area. It was enough for me when I read his motto: "Passing the buck stops here." I don't think he could make it in today's world.

My friend Jim Ward, fire chief of Hollywood, Florida, had a place in Islamorada, part of the Upper Keys. Occasionally we visited Jim and his wife, Kathy, and enjoyed the amenities and laid-back lifestyle the Keys offered. They later visited us in Colorado and bought a summer residence in Crested Butte South. In the Keys, we went out on Jim's boat, the *Fire Escape*. One time we went fishing with him, and I caught my large record fish, a nurse shark. After a couple of scotches that evening, it became known as the world record "Great Gray."

We celebrated the next day by daydreaming at the World Wide Sportsman and having lunch nearby at the Islamorada Fish Company. For many years after we left Florida, we had our Thanksgiving and Christmas food shipped from there. Along with other high-quality ventures like Bass Pro Shops, the Islamorada Fish Company had several locations. Kelli and I always recalled the original one in the Keys when we dined at the one in Denver.

As we traveled near to Ocala, we laughed about my third fire-rookie test. The state of Florida required certification of firefighters. That included carpetbaggers from other states who planned on taking command of any fire operation. If they wanted only to be administrators, a certification wasn't necessary. Why a rookie's test instead of an officer's test, I don't know. Although I had no intention of commanding a fire operation, the certification became a matter of pride for the organization. One could test out for the certification after providing training records documenting the required hours of basic training. I called Bo, then the chief training officer in Wichita, who readily provided paperwork for my three-hundred-plus hours of basic training. After submitting the paperwork, I drove to Ocala and took my written and practical rookie exams.

My coach, Bob Hoecherl, first greeted me at the Bahia Mar station on the evening mentioned earlier. Bob climbed to the top rung of the Fort Lauderdale fire organizational ladder. He and other firefighters have continued improving the system because EMS transport became part of the fire department.

Kelli and I also reminisced about Hurricane Floyd, which ushered us into Florida in 1987, and Hurricane Andrew in 1992, not long before we left. The timing of Hurricane Andrew proved interesting because I had secured my first consulting engagement in Colorado. Jim Ward signed on as my EMS evaluator.

Jim had a friend in the Hurricane Center who'd assured him the storm was headed more northward, so Jim and I, along with Kelli, flew to Colorado. We barely arrived when the storm made a ninety-degree left turn. The fire chiefs of the two largest cities in Broward County had left town. Both departments never missed a beat. That happened because of good plans (developed after ICS), good training, and great personnel. Of course, we endured comments like "Operations went smoothly because you both weren't here."

One of our strongest memories involved a house three blocks from our condo. One morning a story about that nondescript house that Kelli jogged past every morning appeared in the news. The story told how the occupants heard some strange noises, looked out of their back window, and saw a rather large snake slithering under a four-foot fence and making its way toward their house.

As it turned out, the twenty-foot-long, 250-pound python had lived under their house, which sat on the north edge of Hugh Taylor Birch State Park. An overflow of raccoons inhabited the park.

I knew about the raccoons because we had a fire station on the south end of the park, and in the evening tourists fed a gathering pack despite warning signs. The python came out at night, slithered under the fence, and cruised through the heavily wooded park. It occasionally chased a raccoon up a tree and then curled around the tree's base for a little nap. That snake knew what firefighters knew for years. No known record existed of a cat or raccoon skeleton in a tree. They will come down eventually.

According to park rangers, the snake "popped raccoons like marshmallows." The sounds that homeowners kept hearing came from the screams of caught raccoons. After its slow consumption, the self-appointed raccoon population control expert then slithered back to its home under the house.

An enterprising young man in South Florida started a business of relocating those not-so-welcome creatures. The news detailed how that young entrepreneur went under the house and pulled the snake out for capture and removal. Kelli altered her jogging route, and just when memories began fading for her, the offending snake appeared on a nationally televised evening entertainment show. I don't think it helped Kelli when I casually commented, "We can't get away from that animal." Looking back on it, I don't think it helped that I also wondered out loud if the snake had left any youngsters behind.

Nearing the Florida state line, we ticked off a list of all the fun things we experienced. We wouldn't have traded them for anything but looked forward to slower lifestyles, less population density, and those beautiful mountains. As we entered Georgia, we recalled why we left before my contract expired.

Near the end of my contract, the fire chief in Tamarac, Ray Briant, suffered a mild stroke. Except for some minor memory loss, no permanent damage remained, but that event made me think of firefighters who'd remained on the job as long as possible. Many retired and soon died without enjoying retirement. I also paid attention to other firefighters who retired with nothing to occupy their time. They didn't last long either; whereas, those who kept their minds and bodies active did last. That became my motivation for starting my consulting company.

We longed for our Colorado home, so after a brief rest in Biloxi, Mississippi, we drove straight through to Arkansas, alternating driving and sleeping.

In Springdale, Arkansas, we visited the cemetery where Kelli's grandparents were laid to rest. We briefly visited the old house where they used to live, and she recalled vacations and long weekends traveling from Wichita with her parents and two sisters. I met her grandfather only one time when we visited him not long before he died. Kelli confirmed his irreverent sense of humor when she told the story about a pet crow he had that followed him every day to the mailbox and back home. He named the crow Jim.

Kelli remembered another story of riding in a truck with her grandpa headed for Bentonville, Arkansas. They stopped once and helped corral some chickens that had escaped from a crate that fell from a farm truck. As they arrived at a building to pay her grandpa's taxes, he waved at and exchanged greetings with another country fellow. Kelli asked her grandpa for the man's name. Grandpa said, "Oh, that's Sam who lives down the way." Later, she learned Sam's last name—Walton. A positive aspect of his legacy centers on affordable products for middle- and lower-income families.

We talked about ordinary folks who had that entrepreneurial spirit and perseverance to succeed, and knew how to think. Arkansas, Kansas, and Missouri all had people like Sam Walton, with modest beginnings, who achieved unimaginable success by any standard. Two brothers in Wichita started a successful chain of restaurants that served pizza. Their success spawned a Center for Entrepreneurship at Wichita State University. My personal favorite was that Islamorada Fish Company/Bass Pro Shop gentleman who started in Missouri in the back of his father's small retail store. I liked his passion for golf, but his lasting legacy will be all the families he brought together with his company's products and services. He has more than paid his family's gift forward. All three states produced a president as well. After leaving Springdale, we retraced the route Kelli's family took back to Wichita.

We drove straight to my daughter's home and saw my first grandchild. I had grown a beard, and she wouldn't kiss me until I shaved. I've always had fun with and teased those around me that I love. I began by shaving all but a Fu Manchu mustache, and then asked for my kiss, to no avail. I shaved all but a thin mustache, but that didn't work, either. It took a clean shave for my long-awaited kiss. I never grew whiskers again.

After visiting friends and relatives, we headed to our home in Colorado. Arriving late one February afternoon, we tramped through knee-deep snow, depending, of course, on the length of one's legs.

We built fires in fireplaces and turned on all the heat. Going to bed that night, we laughed about leaving the beach for a chilly environment. In the Gunnison Valley, some natives said transients should spend ten winters before being considered a local, so we always counted the remainder of that season as one.

My sleepless thoughts focused on my new role as a consultant to emergency managers. Without the heavy weight of daily responsibility for emergency workers, I could concentrate solely on problem-solving. The one thing I definitely wouldn't miss was the lack of grace that defined many politicians.

33

THE KANSAS KID

My simple business model was based on paying attention to previous consultants. Over the years I noticed that consultants for emergency services were long on academics and short on experience. They generally traveled in a pack of one number cruncher, one partial expert, and one who acted as a tape recorder. The tape recorder person came to town, asked what everyone needed, and then regurgitated that back in a report. The number cruncher supplied statistics for a report, and the partial expert delivered the report. I also remembered my longtime acquaintance Bruno, who provided consulting services for fire command. He described the above pack of consultants as "people who knew how to make love 125 different ways but had no girlfriend."

I came up with an idea for putting together a team of emergency service consultants, all still active in their particular fields, who could use vacation or personal time to work on a project. The concept resembled what I did as fire chief with both fire departments—surrounding myself with people who had a specialized talent or interest in a particular field. I worked with some of the people in Fort Lauderdale, some still in Wichita, and some folks I met along the way. I placed my advertisement, of course, in the International City/ County Management Association monthly magazine, along with those from other consulting firms.

Any interested community submitted a request for proposal (RFP) outlining what type of services they wanted and any other detailed requirements for analysis. I then put together a team of experts in various disciplines and responded to the RFP. That gave various communities access to individuals who attended seminars and stayed current in their fields. I avoided a constant payroll treadmill like other consulting firms and offered our services at a reduced cost. I began using a technique that fit my management style. I used that technique in both my personal and professional life. I knew how and when to use it, but never had a name for it.

I finally found a name for that style in Anchorage, Alaska, with my previous election to the board of directors of the metropolitan fire chiefs' section of the IAFC. The keynote speaker, Dr. Morris Massey, from Colorado University, held a basic premise that sometimes before any behavioral changes could take place, a significant emotional event (SEE) occurred. Dr. Massey said sometimes a SEE needed creating to effect behavioral change. He recalled the story of a student who brought his bicycle into a brand-new building and slid it along a wall, leaving marks. Dr. Massey took the bicycle, threw it outside, and stomped on it. He seemed like my kind of guy.

In management or personal conversation, a SEE could be as simple as raising my voice. Sometimes words needed more volume. At other times an expression of emotion in the form of anger became necessary, all depending on the individual(s) I encountered. People have asked for a description of my management style. I always answered, "It depends on the people with whom I communicate." Because of my education and experience, I thought of myself as a teaching manager, regarding both what and what not to do.

My consulting goal focused on applying my experience and management style to a consulting business that made a thorough evaluation and then told the truth. The way I conveyed truth depended on the individual(s) I encountered.

There will be no grave marker epitaph for me. If I had one, it would read: "Nobody wondered what he was thinking."

My consulting company quickly secured two successive contracts. My simple business model, with a lack of overhead and no payroll treadmill, worked. Not long after the third contract, a fourth came in, and I reevaluated my work schedule. If we wanted that much work, we could've stayed on the beach for more money.

That's when I limited contracts to no more than two or three per year and concentrated on service afterward. I reasoned that assisting in implementing our recommendations at no additional cost would improve our references and success rate.

That business strategy worked so well that our competition began taking notice. We lost a couple of bids and couldn't understand why until checking with the communities. They couldn't understand how we provided the same or better level of service at such a reduced cost. They checked our references, and all agreed they were superior. As one old bureaucrat told me, "I don't understand how two companies can provide a Cadillac, but only one charges the price of a Ford."

No amount of reasoning helped him see we sold a service, not a product. I gave up trying and started adding "feel-good" money to our fee. If more money made them feel good, it would make me feel good too.

Some of our competition participated in a program that involved additional work after the initial contract. Competitors would describe for communities how to implement their recommendations. I eliminated the need for an implementation contract by pulling all recommendations from a report and placing them on a recommendation spreadsheet. I included columns for recommendations, a timeline for completion, associated costs, who had responsibility for implementation, and priority ranking for each recommendation. Besides cutting out additional work, we made financially and politically feasible recommendations.

I analyzed the differences between the public and private sectors. The private sector asked, "What's my investment, and what's my return on investment?" The public sector asked, "What's my investment, what's my return on investment, and how does it look politically?" That last part of the equation became a tough variable to understand.

One of my graduate classes dealt with organizational behavior and involved case studies, but all those case studies and reading materials focused on the private sector. Every time the tenured professor graded my papers and analyzed the case afterward, I pointed out why that wouldn't work in the public sector or a unionized environment. Silly me, I thought the purpose of a collegiate environment was encouraging the free exchange of ideas. Those disagreements with the professor probably explained why I received only a B for what to think.

I paid attention to the study materials, and what I took away from the class helped me analyze any organization, then apply personal and political touches. The more clinical part of a review involved two stages: first, analyzing an organizational chart as well as all policies and procedures; and second, interviewing political decision makers as well as rank and file employees.

Most educated and experienced individuals did an adequate job of the first part, analyzing, but few gained valuable information through an interview process. I gained individuals' trust quickly and guaranteed confidentiality. It's key to identify the patterns that separate organizational from personal concerns, while never ignoring personal concerns. My competition couldn't compete in that second area, because they didn't have the same experience as I did.

A roadblock appeared in RFPs requiring multiple study samples identical to the one requested. I countered that anyone given enough time could produce multiple studies, but successful completion of recommendations mattered more. Also, every community had a different financial and political makeup. I recommended that community members concentrate on reference checks from previous engagements by asking how many recommendations were implemented, and added that since we provided custom-tailored work, all studies differed. Any consulting company could make endless recommendations, but if just a few became implemented, the study seemed of little value.

The next roadblock included an RFP requirement for $1,000,000 in errors-and-omissions insurance. That was difficult at first because only licensed professionals such as engineers could obtain that kind of insurance. I finally found a company that originated in Wichita, Insurance Management Associates, that provided the insurance. They had an office in Denver. Anytime an insurance requirement appeared, I added on that cost, like the feel-good money.

Because I was known as a change agent and truth teller, my company's reputation began building. The word must have gotten out about the doctor's last name on my birth certificate—Earp. Mom told me of the delivery doctor's old age at the time of my birth, so he was possibly related to Wyatt. Wyatt's the guy who went from Wichita to Dodge City to Arizona, then to Gunnison. I went from Wichita to Fort Lauderdale to Gunnison.

Occasionally client department members said, "The Kansas Kid's coming to town." Also, the ringtone on my cell phone played my favorite song, "A Change Is Gonna Come," by Sam Cooke. The thought of coming changes, delivered by a known change agent who shot from the lip, must've given cause for concern.

Over the next several years I maintained as much work as needed for paying my health insurance premiums. That minimal amount of work allowed for more time at home with all our summertime guests.

Like many in the Gunnison Valley, we jokingly said that we had nine months of winter and three months of visitors.

Our families, former members of both fire departments, including Captain Ajax, and other professional associates have spent time with us. My pals from the Baggers, Harry Diezel and Dick Moreno, have visited. I felt closer to Dicky Moreno because he was our expert on cultural perversity. After that first visit, Harry called once in a while and talked about getting together again, but mostly he just talked. He wanted a meeting while on some other business that already paid for his travel expenses because he was a cheapskate.

Harry served briefly on the city council in Virginia Beach, Virginia. Charley Rule ran for the council in Camp Douglas, Wisconsin, where he retired. Charley said he placed brochures in bars, and his opponent placed his in churches. Charley told me he appealed to both candidates' constituencies. I worked with Charley anytime we did business in the Great Lakes region. I stayed in touch with him until the end of his life. His final conversation included stories about harassing the nursing staff. He wanted any contributions after his passing sent to a fallen firefighter's memorial. My company donated in his name.

My company provided emergency services consulting for fire, EMS, police, and emergency management departments. The human resources specialist I chose, Arlette Steinberger, had a reputation for being nitpicky and uncompromising concerning sound personnel practices. Having worked with her in Fort Lauderdale, I knew that was true. Her nickname had three letters, SFB. The first two letters stood for South Florida.

My office when I was in Fort Lauderdale had shared a common hallway with personnel, so my mornings always started with a casual mosey through their offices, greeting Arlette along the way. Any organization had a key information center. In Fort Lauderdale, all information flowed through personnel. Labor relations honchos, Scott and John, knew everything that happened. I stayed plugged in to organizations because the information was critical for managing or even being a successful part of any organization.

In Wichita, the information center was the budget office. In addition to living by the golden rule ("Them that have the gold make the rules"), they signed off on most expenditure requests. All management decisions had a budget implication, so I spent a lot of time with the budget director, who reported to the finance director.

As a young lieutenant at Station 2, I always took my meals at the firefighters' table and spoke their language. Staying connected to all levels in any organization produced no surprises and gave time for thoughtful decision-making.

When my company did police studies, I needed an analytical police chief who spoke police language. I worked with an individual I met in Wisconsin. We lost a bid on consolidation of several departments on the North Shore, but that let me meet the Whitefish Bay police chief, Gary Mikulec. Gary was stoutly built and had closely cropped hair, eyelids that narrowed when he focused, and a brow that raised when he questioned something he'd just heard. All those features gave him a no-nonsense appearance that belied his great sense of humor and compassion. To me, a compassionate culture separated great police departments from good ones.

Gary, like my friend Richard LaMunyon, also had great management skills. Gary was an interim Whitefish Bay town manager. He shared my philosophy about telling the truth. If a department did the right thing, that was noted. If they didn't, that was also noted. Gary's analytical skills, coupled with his knowledge of computer and dispatch systems, seemed unequaled from a police perspective.

When it came time for Gary to retire and move on, I introduced him to a city manager, Carl Metzger, in Ankeny, Iowa. Gary became their police chief and built a first-class police department complete with state-of-the-art training facilities.

Carl had somewhat of a Gregory Peck appearance and a personality like Atticus Finch in the movie *To Kill a Mockingbird.* He was kind and considerate, and did the right thing in all management decisions and recommendations. Carl graduated from the WSU urban affairs program. We occasionally visited when he spent summers in Buena Vista, Colorado. Carl left Ankeny and, after a couple of years with Des Moines, retired. He was one of the most professional city managers I encountered. He cared about employees and always tried developing subordinates. Managers like Carl were best described as visionaries. They managed for the future rather than reacting to it on arrival. The best ICS commanders managed emergencies that way as well.

Gary remained in Ankeny until 2018, then retired. He only had three phobias in life: flying, confined spaces, and lightning. I tried helping him overcome his flying issue by booking as many flight changes as possible and comforted him before entering an enclosed MRI machine for a kidney stone problem. Gary never thanked me for helping place him in Iowa, where heavy thunderstorms were commonplace. Desensitizing should've helped.

I could recount many stories of the different communities we provided services for, but that wouldn't be fair. If they did everything right, there wouldn't have been a need for our services. The worst fire department we encountered had no standard operating procedures (SOPs), not even one that suggested wearing an air tank and mask when entering a hazardous atmosphere. When asked why, they replied, "Without SOPs, we can't be held responsible for not following them."

A dentist once asked if I clenched my teeth. "Only when I witness stupidity," I immediately replied. Hearing the reason for no SOPs became a teeth-clenching moment.

One of the more interesting characters I met was a blind fire chief. The chief asked if I had ever worked with a blind fire chief before. "No, but I have worked with some who couldn't see." That got a good laugh out of him.

The best-managed mayor/council forms of government resulted from mayors listening to city administrators and not sacrificing good management for politics. The form of government didn't seem as important as the individuals who filled those positions, but in most cases, professional managers in manager/council forms of government managed successful organizations. In manager/council forms of government, usually established by charter ordinance and a vote of the citizens, a city manager had absolute authority over all personnel matters. Although different communities had variations, generally council members had authority over one employee—a city manager. Still, some politicians tried mucking up the works. If a council member became unhappy with an employee, like a fire chief who enforced fire codes, they put pressure on a city manager to "deal" with the employee.

I had that experience with Politician in Wichita. He asked me one time if the city manager ever disciplined me. I told him that he hadn't, and Politician walked away. As always, I later told the city manager about the encounter, and he confirmed that Politician had been pressuring him. Gene Denton, like me, didn't respond well to threats and was devoted to the manager/council form of government. He easily moved to another job, but I'm sure the pressure for some city managers, in similar situations, must've been overwhelming.

When political interference with professional management didn't fit politicians' needs, they claimed that was an area that fell under the purview of a city manager. If they couldn't get a political consensus on their pet projects, they put pressure on a city manager to accomplish their goals. Some politicians also hid behind a manager/council form of government from political pressure of their own. If they received pressure from donors as a result of budget cuts, they said, "Well, the city manager and staff recommended those budget reductions," or "I tried having your project included in the budget, but staff said we couldn't afford it." I knew if some catastrophe happened as a result of budget cuts some politician would say, "Well, the fire chief didn't object to those cuts," or better yet, "The fire chief recommended those cuts." If something tragic happened as a result of unenforced fire codes, I knew who would get blamed, thus my response to Politician in the city hall cafeteria.

I had little patience for those politicians. I did have the patience for and appreciated the other 99 percent of politicians who stayed out of management and concentrated on policy matters. With few exceptions, I have no regrets about my lack of patience and any actions that followed.

One Saturday morning during my 2014 winter visit to Wichita, before my granddaughter's WSU graduation ceremonies, I was having breakfast with Bo, LJ, Pink, Maxi, and Bill. Bill, one of those innocent bystanders, retold the story of the time Bo placed a hard plastic water-filled container on top of a ceiling fan blade in the fire station kitchen. He wondered how many times it would go around before falling. The answer: one, before it landed on the calm hero lieutenant sitting below. He watched the entire process with his normally cool demeanor. He responded, however, by throwing his coffee cup at Bo, who ran out of the kitchen. The cup shattered against a metal door jam.

Everyone has a limit. I always reach mine a little quicker than most people, but I've paid attention, and I'm still learning how to think.

34

*P*ATIENCE/*A*DAPTATION

Patience that I lacked in my professional life came more easily when interacting with my grandchildren. I needed patience and found it when I taught my son, daughter, and granddaughters how to snow ski. Because of Colorado's proximity to Wichita, my granddaughters, Allie, Katie, and Chloe, came out almost every winter. All three of them learned to ski, but my daughter noted that I had a lot more patience with them than I had with her. She recalled the time she fell and experienced some difficulty clearing snow from her boots to reattach the skis. She claimed that I said something like "Stop whining, buck it up, and let's get on with it."

I recalled something like "Oh, my darling, you have fallen yet again. Let me clean the snow from your boots and help you up so we can all have fun again," as I said to my granddaughters. Looking back on it, perhaps I wasn't as patient with my son and daughter, but I aimed at reinforcing training instructions such as "Don't open the camper window while the vehicle is in motion."

My biggest concern for a beginning skier's safety focused on slowing their speed while traversing down mountain slopes without inhibiting the beginner's progress. That was also a goal when managing. My answer came when I noticed a man with his youngster finish their last run. The man had a green waist harness attached to his youngster with reins on either side. I remembered my mother telling me the story of her difficulty in keeping me by her side. While Mom shopped for a particular item, I did some forward scouting. On one of my reconnaissance missions, I wandered out of a store and down the street. In the early 1950s, police officers walked a downtown beat now called a "patrol area." The term "cop" means constable on patrol. With help from a local beat cop, Mom finally found me. That frantic desperation led to a chest harness complete with leash. That new green skiing apparatus I saw didn't have the stigma of a chest harness but proved just as effective.

I now have great-grandchildren, and I'm considering a return to the skiing instruction effort for the fourth generation. That would have first and fourth generations skiing together, and patience will prevail. Just in case, I will purchase a green waist harness, for me.

My company became part of the IAFC consulting services, and we sold our Colorado home and moved to Texas. I originally built the large Colorado home as a magnet for my children, grandchildren, and great-grandchildren. It worked both in the winter for skiing and in summer for hiking, fishing, golfing, and rafting. But the size of the home and extreme cold in winter made us consider a downsized move to a more temperate annual climate. We wanted an area that had recreational amenities and still attracted family and friends. That led us to South Texas, where three months of summer heat are better than nine months of winter cold. The prevailing southern breezes over the Gulf coastal waters temper the heat and a summer water park might still act as a good magnet. I'm sure winters will bring the most company. Former fire department brothers Tom Weber and Maxi Winsor have already visited.

I look forward to more vacation visits with my grandchildren. It's fun watching their different stages of growth without the responsibility of shaping how they turn out. I've enjoyed the same relationship with my two fire department families. As usual, I have a saying: "Retired chiefs should stay that way." Only the current chief has responsibility for dealing with internal and external political pressures placed on a department. The departments are no longer my responsibility, but I still enjoy hearing about their growth and development. I empathize with their organizational bumps and bruises and revel in their successes. I didn't want my name on the notification list when some of the members pass on because we spent so much time on keeping them safe and healthy. It was too depressing thinking about what I might have done differently, thereby extending their lives.

I also don't think as much about what I could've done better as a father or grandfather. Some people never get over an imperfect past or present and use that as an excuse to play out their victim drama games of unhappiness. They walk around looking like the back of their hand is glued to their forehead. I spend time appreciating my past and present and look forward to any future blessings. My only responsibility is to focus on having a good time when family and friends get together. My adaptation to more patience results from less responsibility. It's fun being gentler with myself and others.

We are all products of our life's experience. Our values, beliefs, and how we see our experience are shaped by family, friends, people we admire, and institutional participation. My father didn't have to worry about leaving me at age thirteen without a fatherly influence because he already did his job of instilling characteristics such as self-reliance and a strong work ethic. Although I missed him as a role model, Dad's death set me on a path to independence. It became clear real quick that if I wanted something like a vehicle, I'd better work and start saving money. My father's obligation to his family allowed me to see my obligation to two fire department families. If one member had been mortally wounded, I would've felt as if I failed in my duty to protect them.

With respect to institutions, we attended church and understood the importance of values like integrity and caring for other people. The role religion played in my life proved substantial because participation took place during my formative years. Faith became one of the longest-lasting gifts of religion. Along with reinforcing church-taught values, my mother and father provided the basis for my two favorite human emotions, love and humor.

The fire service let me live my values, and freely express my emotions. No profession other than the fire service would have given me the kind of job satisfaction I experienced. In addition to religion and the fire service, education had the largest institutional influence on my life, specifically improving my reasoning ability.

Family, friends, people we admire, institutions, professions, and life experience in general all provide opportunities for learning. There are both good and bad things associated with different sources of learning. Faith and hope can lead to eternal optimism, but there's a fine line between eternal optimism and being delusional. Paying attention is how one separates the wheat from the chaff. This approach also allows one to look at disagreeable people, or even unlikable people, and ask a question: *If everything about my background, DNA, and history replicated people I disagree with or dislike, would I see things the same way as they do?* This approach might provide an avenue to open communication on substance rather than appearance. Different people or groups of people require different approaches when communicating or interacting. We can't communicate or interact with people based solely on our own values and beliefs.

I began thinking about my past experiences when I visited the Firefighters Museum in Wichita several years ago with my son, daughter-in-law, and grandsons, Jared and Jack. That building was the last horse-drawn steamer facility owned by the city. Its demise wasn't from a lack of trying, because a couple of high-level bureaucrats tried selling the building to a law firm. While still fire chief, I stopped that by unleashing the hysterical society on them. We demonstrated that we could provide continual upkeep on the building. Maxi fixed the brick on the outside, and so began the museum. The retired firefighters have taken that building so much further than anyone could have imagined. It's now part of a Fallen Firefighters Memorial, where honor is paid in formal ceremonies every year. Knowledge and appreciation of the past seems important for moving into the future. That's been a basis for these memoir episodes.

The most inspirational person in my life, my mother, passed away four years ago in Arizona, where she lived with my sister Lisa, and near my sister Karla. Both beautiful women came the nearest to our mother's example. Mom meant so much to me because of her early influence on my life. I appreciated traveling to Arizona and visiting one last time. A hospice nurse met with the family on the day before our scheduled return trip to Colorado. She told us it was a matter of weeks, so we should convey our final thoughts including any negative questions. That let me tease Mom once again. Shortly thereafter, Kelli, Karla, and I sat visiting with Mom. I smiled and asked, "Do you remember the time you put a dog chest harness with a leash on me before you shopped?" She looked quizzically at me, then Karla.

"Did you put a harness on Jimmy?"

Then Mom smiled. "He wouldn't stay near me and kept running off. I warned him several times. The last time a police officer helped find him. That was the last straw." We all laughed.

Before we left, I walked over to where Mom sat and knelt down in front of our sweet matriarch. I took hold of her hands. "I love you." I got up, leaned over, and gave her a final kiss. She gave me a final smiling image.

During the journey back to Colorado, I reflected on some of our final phone conversations. Mom always retold the story of how she led a serpentine dance on a cruise with all my sisters. That seemed interesting because she raised me as a Baptist and sent me to school with a note that exempted me from square dancing. There was an old joke about Baptists not wanting their children having premarital sex because they feared it would lead to dancing. My personal life substantiated that belief.

During our final conversations Mom talked more about the afterlife. I always brought her back to the five living generations. I usually mentioned something about my longevity goals, and right on cue she would say, "You do know, Son, the Bible says we know not the hour or the day."

She always fell right into my trap. "I know, Mom, and that's why it's important to concentrate on celebrating life each day and let God think about our mortality." We repeated those words at least two times during our fifteen-minute conversations.

I admired how far Mom came from the backwoods of Missouri, where her memory would often return to her first new pair of shoes. I can still see the delight in her eyes and smile on her face. That image quickly turned to sadness when she recalled how someone stole those precious shoes. Almost immediately a shoulder-shrugging move of resignation was followed by two sentences. "Oh well, I guess someone needed those shoes more than I did. I hope they enjoyed them as much as I did."

There are a couple of areas where I've rebelled against Mom's values, character, and beliefs. Besides our patience levels, there's one other area where we differed—forgiveness. Her complete willingness to help other people at her own expense sometimes let others take advantage of her. Her religious belief had her "turn the other cheek." I couldn't do that and never again trusted someone who wronged me or wronged someone I cared about. As usual, though, I always learned something and moved on. Forgiveness seemed worth at least considering if I put myself in a wrongdoer's place. Although it's no excuse for bad actions, those unforgiven people were products of poorly formed character and values.

Although I've enjoyed reflecting on the past, the future holds more excitement regarding a new environment, new acquaintances, and more time with loved ones. Kelli and I enjoy Texas winters, but we will miss summers in the Gunnison Valley. Recognizing the Gunnison Valley political landscape was easy because the valley was divided into two groups. The north end included the ski area and the south end, except for the university, included the more conservative folk. Two living presidents have visited the valley. One stayed at the north end of the valley, and one stayed at the south end. However, the entire valley was united in protecting the environment, specifically its most precious resource—water.

A word of caution if talking to my favorite class of people in the Gunnison Valley—ranchers: they don't like being called "farmers." I did have some fun with one rancher I know.

It started with my question, "Do you grow your hay crop?"

"Of course," he replied.

Then I told him about the acres of hay I helped a dairy farmer cut, rake, bale, and store, but I didn't recall ever herding a crop to the barn.

We settled in the Gunnison Valley twenty-eight years ago because of planning considerations like recreation, medical facilities, and an airport. We got a bonus because Gunnison was home to Western State Colorado University, formerly Western State College. Communities with colleges and universities are always more diverse and vibrant.

One of the current debates in academic and scientific communities focuses on artificial intelligence (AI). The concern centers on what happens when nonhumans learn how to think. Some people and groups should be concerned when more humans learn how to think. To me, humans that know what to think have AI.

Most educational institutions offer good learning opportunities. In school, as in life, paying attention helps separate the people who teach *what* to think from the ones who teach *how* to think. I've made four observations:

1. People of substance who know *how* to think support their position with facts and welcome open debate, while appearance-oriented people tell others *what* to think, sometimes by changing the subject, evoking emotion, and quashing open debate.
2. Appearance-oriented people stop and argue with each other over a path they take to achieve a common goal, while people of substance keep their eye on the goal.
3. Appearance-oriented people characterize other people and their motives to draw attention away from other people's substance and ideas.
4. Appearance-oriented people lacking in substance and character denigrate others while people of substance spend time improving their own lives.

These four observations are good for all people, not only teachers.

§

There's no such thing as midwestern values, only values. Like my golf game, there is good, bad, and ugly everywhere. People of substance and character who have values and know how to think aren't in one particular location, race, religion, gender, national origin, sexual orientation, or ideology. Paying attention helps identify them.

My sister Jeanie and brother, Brent, live in Texas. They are both good people and I love them dearly, like I do all my siblings. Hopefully we can all spend more time together.

Now with more patience, I'm adapting and looking forward to spending time in Texas because Texas bills itself as a "whole other country." I know it's true because of a visit I paid to the Royal Gorge. Flags from countries all over the world flew along with one from the Lone Star State. If I get bored, I might apply to the Department of State for the Texas ambassadorship. My choice of dress and an embassy in South Texas are nonnegotiable.

Concerning my ambassadorship appearance, I still have my 4X Beaver John B. Stetson hat. My jeans are the boot-cut style. I like the boot cut because it reminds me of a slight bell-bottom. I like the bell-bottom look because of the pants my father wore while in the navy, where bell-bottoms originated. I don't need placement at the top of a pay scale, but they must also permit my wearing of deck shoes for state affairs and sneakers of my choice for daily affairs. Last, they must accept my new top clothier. His name is Thomas. I believe he's from the Bahamas.

Whatever you say or do will be far too much for some and never enough for others—press on!

Jim Sparr holds a BA in education and a master's degree in urban affairs from Wichita State University. As an adjunct instructor, he taught fire science classes at Hutchinson Kansas Community College and Wichita State University. Jim has worked as a fire chief in Wichita, Kansas and Fort Lauderdale, Florida. He has also owned and operated a consulting company specializing in fire, police, EMS, and emergency management. Jim is a past president of the Metropolitan Fire Chiefs and a lifetime member of the International Association of Fire Chiefs.

CPSIA information can be obtained
at www.ICGtesting.com
Printed in the USA
LVHW090806060420
652293LV00026B/276